DATE DUE			
JAN 09 '01			
JAN 31 '01			

12/00

JACKSON COUNTY
Library Services

HEADQUARTERS
413 West Main Street
Medford, Oregon 97501

The — GRAND OLE OPRY

Country Christmas Album

The

GRAND OLE OPRY®

Country Christmas
Album

*Celebrating America's Favorite Holiday
with the Legends of Country Music*

EDITED BY JOE LAYDEN

BERKLEY BOULEVARD BOOKS
NEW YORK

THE GRAND OLE OPRY® COUNTRY CHRISTMAS ALBUM

A Berkley Boulevard Book
Published by The Berkley Publishing Group
A division of Penguin Putnam Inc.
375 Hudson Street
New York, New York 10014

Grand Ole Opry® is a registered trademark and is used under license from Gaylord
Entertainment Company.
Book design by Pauline Neuwirth, Neuwirth & Associates, Inc.
Interior photos: pages xii, 2, 10, 14, 30, 48, 53, 62, 78, 82, 85, 94, 106, 118, 128, 152,
162, 170, 188, 192, 214, 220 by Alan L. Mayor; pages 6, 16, 19, 20, 56, 76, 93, 124, 136,
140, 164, 176, 198, 201, 202 by Donnie Beauchamp; page 24 by Senor McGuire;
pages 36, 146 by Jerry Gaza; page 42 by Reta DeGraff; page 70 by Bill Thorup, © 2000
Mercury Records; page 88 by Exley; pages 100, 105 by Ron Davis; page 112 used by
permission of Jimmy C. Newman; page 158 used by permission of Del Reeves;
page 182 by Nancy Andrews; page 208 by Mark Tucker.

First edition: October 2000

The Penguin Putnam Inc. World Wide Web site address is
http://www.penguinputnam.com

Library of Congress Cataloging-in-Publication Data

The grand ole opry country Christmas album : celebrating America's favorite holiday
with the legends of country music / edited by Joe Layden.
         p. cm.
      ISBN 0-425-17652-5
      1. Country music—History and criticism. 2. Country musicians. 3. Christmas—
Anecdotes. 4. Christmas stories, American. I. Layden, Joseph, 1959–

   ML3524 .G69 2000
   781.723'1642—dc21
                                                                00-031221

Printed in the United States of America

10 9 8 7 6 5 4 3 2 1

Contents

Acknowledgments

*I*T ISN'T EASY to get forty artists to agree on anything; however, the musicians who were interviewed for this book and who provided the stories that make it interesting were unanimous in their view that it was a worthwhile endeavor. They invested a substantial amount of time and energy—without receiving any compensation—and for that I am immensely grateful. Without their cooperation, obviously, this book would not have been possible.

In addition to the artists themselves, a number of people from the Grand Ole Opry offered invaluable support and guidance, and were instrumental in keeping the project on track, most notably Pete Fisher, Jerry Strobel, Dan Rogers, Gina Keltner and Cookie Callahan.

Without the help of a small army of publicists, agents and managers, this would have been a much slimmer volume. So, thanks to Clark Beavon, Jenny Bohler, Woody Bowles, Sandy Brokaw, Dian Cash, Mike Chamberlain, Marc Dottore, Marty Martel, Joy McReynolds and Euneta Oswald, and to everyone else who works behind the scenes.

A special thanks to my editor, Denise Silvestro, whose enormous patience was greatly appreciated, and to her assistant, Martha Bushko. As always, thanks to my agent, Frank Weimann of the Literary Group, and to Jessica Wainwright and Frank Coffey, who introduced me to the project.

Introduction

*I*S THERE A time of year that evokes stronger feelings than Christmas? For most of us, the holiday season is at once a whirlwind of activity and a period of quiet reflection. Amidst the frantic shopping and traveling, the festive partying, there are moments of intense nostalgia, for there is no other time, no other holiday, that tugs so firmly at our hearts and minds.

Each year, as Christmas draws near, anticipation mixes with melancholy. The first gentle snowfall, the familiar refrain of a favorite Christmas song played against the backdrop of a crackling and hissing hearth, the intoxicating aroma of a fresh batch of cookies, a newly cut spruce tree—all of these are capable not only of putting us in the proper spirit of things, but of whisking us away to another time and place. Like the Ghost of Christmas Past, the sights and sounds and smells of the season take us by the hand and lead us on a spiritual and emotional journey. How easily the years slip away! How vividly we recall the past and the holidays of our youth.

And just as easily we return. We join friends and relatives and create new memories, new traditions. Because that, on one level at least, is what Christmas is all about: giving, sharing, loving, remembering.

The Grand Ole Opry Country Christmas Album is both a celebration of the holiday season and a heartfelt Christmas card from some of the biggest stars in country music. Like the rest of us, the artists featured on these pages have powerful memories of Christmas, and they've been kind enough to share them with you, the fans, who represent nothing less than their extended family. The stories, of course, are as diverse as the artists themselves. They are stories of family and friends, of life and love and loss, of church and children . . . and, of course, music.

If there is a thread that runs through the fabric of this book, that binds one tale to the next, one artist to another, it is, appropriately enough, music. In some cases the song is in the forefront, as in the tender story of Travis Tritt, who recalls the joyous day in his fourteenth year when he received from his father a new guitar for Christmas—despite the fact that his dad really didn't approve of the boy's infatuation with music; or in the story of Sonny Osborne, the banjo-playing younger half of the legendary bluegrass duo the Osborne Brothers, whose signature song, "Rocky Top," was released on Christmas Day in 1967.

And in other cases, music echoes sweetly in the background: Holly Dunn remembering the Southwestern feasts of her childhood, during which she and her brother would invariably "do a little pickin'"; Dana Williams, bass player for Diamond Rio, wistfully replacing his father's old Jackie Gleason Christmas collection on compact disc; Trisha Yearwood dreaming of the day she would hit it big and drive home in a brand-new truck for her dad, windows down, her new CD shouting from the dash, proudly announcing her arrival.

Not all of the stories are happy. Some are poignant, some are sad, some are endearingly odd and some are humorous. But each, in its own way, is truly memorable; each provides a small, clear window into the soul of the artist, for there is perhaps no time when we are more vulnerable, more open . . . more human . . . than at Christmastime.

—JOE LAYDEN

BILL
Anderson

I N   H I S   N E A R L Y   forty-year career, "Whisperin' Bill" Anderson has quietly compiled one of the most impressive and eclectic resumes in country music. A prolific singer, songwriter, producer, businessman and actor, he slides gracefully from one segment of the entertainment business to another, rarely pausing long enough to take a breath.

Bill grew up in Commerce, Georgia, and graduated with a degree in journalism from the University of Georgia. After a brief stint as a newspaper reporter, he took a job as a disc jockey, and he's been involved with music ever since.

Few Nashville artists have equaled Bill's productivity. Over the years he's released more than fifty albums and won more than fifty BMI songwriting awards, more than anyone else in the history of country music. He's placed nearly seventy-five of his own singles on the country music charts; hundreds more have been recorded by a wide range of artists, including Brenda Lee, Eddy Arnold, Conway Twitty, Roy Acuff, Vince Gill and Jerry Lee Lewis. Among Bill's most recognizable tunes are "City Lights," "When Two Worlds Collide," "Tips of My Fingers" and "I May Never Get to Heaven."

Although Bill's gift for songwriting is obvious, it is hardly his only talent. He's hosted a game show for ABC and been a performer on the soap opera *One Life to Live.* He's also hosted a number of television shows for The Nashville Network (TNN), including *Fandango* and *Opry Backstage.* Bill put his journalistic tools to good use in 1989 with the publication of his autobiography, *Whisperin' Bill.* Four years later, he penned *I Hope You're Living as High on the Hog as the Pig You Turned Out to Be.*

A member of the Nashville Songwriters Association Hall of Fame and the Georgia Music Hall of Fame, Bill has been cited by *Billboard* magazine as one of country music's three all-time greatest country music songwriters (along with Hank Williams and Harlan Howard). He joined the Grand Ole Opry on July 15, 1961.

Brad Paisley visits Bill backstage.

The Grand Ole Opry Country Christmas Album

Bill

Remembers . . .

I would say that the event that happened at Christmastime that is most memorable for me actually happened when I was an adult rather than when I was a child. It was the Christmas of 1969. I had been in Nashville about ten years at that point. And I had two young daughters. My oldest daughter, Terri, was about eight years old, and my youngest daughter, Jenni, was about four. I was going through a divorce from their mother, and they had come over to spend several days prior to Christmas. I was experiencing all of this guilt stuff that I guess you feel at a time like that. You know—you're going through a divorce, and you don't want to hurt your kids, and you're feeling guilty, and you're having all of this vast range of emotions. And, of course, you're trying to get the career going at the same time. In other words, things just seem to be kind of closing in on you from all sides.

On the night of December 23, the night before Christmas Eve, I was tucking my little girls in bed, and . . . I don't know . . . for some reason that particular night it just seemed to be hitting me really hard. It was just me and my two daughters in the house and I had tried to make the last couple of days as much fun for them and as pleasant for them as I possibly could.

But that night, I remember, as I was tucking them in, something remarkable happened. When we were all still together as a family, we had kind of started a tradition at our house. Every Christmas Eve I would read to the girls. I would read "The Night Before Christmas," and then I would read them the Christmas story from the Bible. It was something we had started at a very early age, and we had continued to do it as they grew. We had done it as a family, and it was very important to us. So I had done that on this night. I had read them the Christmas stories and I was tucking my girls in bed, and my heart was pretty heavy. I thought, Golly, I'm just a total failure at this father business. And just as I tucked my youngest daughter in bed, she looked up at me and she gave me the biggest, most wonderful smile that you can imagine. She reached up and she put her arms around my neck, and she said, "Daddy, Terri and I are so lucky." And I said, "Why is that, honey?" And she said, "Because we have two houses where we're loved."

Man . . . I can hardly tell that story without getting choked up. I have carried that memory with me for a whole lot of Christmases, let me tell you, because it was probably the best Christmas present I ever got.

Bill's
Favorite Christmas Song

I don't mean for this to sound conceited, and I hope it doesn't, but Steve Wariner and I wrote a song three or four years ago that Alabama recorded in their Christmas album, called "Christmas in Your Arms." It's a love song. I don't know that I would say it's my favorite Christmas song, but it's one I love to sing, and I sing it a lot on the Opry. It's kind of a personal song to me.

ERNIE
Ashworth

WHEN ERNIE ASHWORTH was a boy, growing up around the cotton fields of Huntsville, Alabama, he dreamed of performing on the stage of the Grand Ole Opry. That he made that dream come true is testament not only to his talent as a songwriter, but to a rare combination of determination and drive.

Ernie arrived in Nashville in the early 1950s and quickly hooked up with a band playing the local nightclub circuit. Although he was a pretty fair guitarist and vocalist, it was Ernie's skill as a songwriter that first caught the eye of the music industry—no surprise, really, considering he wrote his first songs before he even knew how to play the guitar.

Before long Ernie's music was attracting the likes of Little Jimmy Dickens, Carl Smith and Johnny Horton. When Acuff-Rose Publishing signed Ernie to an exclusive writing contract, it appeared as though his career would take off. But it didn't quite work out that way.

In 1957, when business slowed for him, Ernie was forced to return to Huntsville and take a job at Redstone Arsenal. Certain that another break would come, he continued to write songs and play music. And his diligence was rewarded. In 1960 Ernie signed a recording contract with Decca Records, for which he recorded the Top 10 hits "Each Moment" and "You Can't Pick a Rose in December." In 1963 he released his biggest single, the No.1 hit "Talk Back Trembling Lips," on Hickory Records, which remained on the national country music charts for thirty-six weeks. The following year his greatest dream was fulfilled when he was invited to join the cast of the Grand Ole Opry on March 7. Ernie had a string of Top 10 hits in the sixties, and later became the owner of a country music radio station in Ardmore, Tennessee.

Ernie
Remembers . . .

I grew up during the Depression era, a time when no one had much of anything. We were a poor family, and most everyone around us was poor, too. My dad worked in a cotton mill, and I grew up in Lincoln Village, a little town in which all the homes were actually owned by the cotton mill, and everyone who lived there worked at the mill. It wasn't far from Huntsville, Alabama. We lived there for several years, and I remember Christmas in that village being very different from what Christmas is today. It wasn't about getting a lot of presents or anything like that. It was about families getting together and supporting each other, showing their love for each other. We got maybe one present, and that one present had to last the whole year. I guess some people probably didn't get anything at all, but Daddy always tried to get us something.

We had a big family—I had one brother and three sisters—so it was hard for my daddy. But he always put food on the table and clothes on our back, I don't know how. Sometimes our shirts were made out of flour sacks. But Christmastime was always a happy time because we were together. As a family. Sharing Christmas dinner and taking care of each other. We had 364 days of not-too-happy times, because compared to now, there just wasn't any money. But we had one very happy day. It was a special day for all of us

JIM ED

Brown

JIM ED BROWN'S interest in music was kindled when he was just a boy growing up in rural Arkansas. On Saturday nights his entire family would cluster around a battery-powered radio and listen to broadcasts from the Grand Ole Opry. Across the miles and through the Arkansas night, Jim Ed could feel the pull of the Opry stage. He began harmonizing with his older sister, Maxine, and before long the duo were performing on local radio shows. When Jim Ed was in college, he and Maxine became featured performers on the *Barnyard Frolic*, a popular show broadcast out of KLRA in Little Rock. They also wrote "Looking Back to See," which became their first hit single.

With the addition of Jim Ed's younger sister, Bonnie, the Browns became a trio, and soon they had their first Top 10 hit, "Here Today and Gone Tomorrow." The No. 1 singles "I Take the Chance" and "I Heard the Bluebird Sing" followed. The group's biggest hit was "The Three Bells," released in 1959, which sold more than a million copies and became the first country tune ever to reach the top of the pop and rhythm-and-blues charts.

When Bonnie and Maxine retired from the group in the mid-1960s, Jim Ed went out on his own. He charted with several songs, including "Pop-a-Top Again," "Southern Loving" and "Morning." In 1976 Jim Ed welcomed a new partner in Helen Cornelius, and the two found an eager audience for their work, which included the No. 1 hits "I Don't Want to Have to Marry You" and "Saying Hello, Saying I Love You, Saying Goodbye." More recently Jim Ed has been the host of the TNN shows *You Can Be a Star* and *Going Our Way*.

Jim Ed Brown joined the cast of the Grand Ole Opry on August 12, 1963.

Jim Ed
Remembers . . .

Christmas in our house always revolved around family, as it does in most homes, I guess. Our holidays were simple because we were very poor. This was down in south Arkansas in the late 1930s, and everybody around us was poor. But you know, the funny thing was, you didn't feel like you were missing out because nobody else had anything either.

My father was in the logging business. He didn't have any high-tech equipment, just a wagon and a team of mules and horses. He worked mostly for a man who owned a sawmill nearby. Back then, living down South, the sons were expected to grow up and follow in their fathers' footsteps. And that's what most of them did. That being the case, when I was five or six, I started helping out. I couldn't do much, but I was able to help him harness the team, feed the animals, that sort of thing. I understood from a very early age just how hard my daddy worked. It seemed like he was always working, day and night, all year long, even on Sundays. But he would always take off Christmas Day, and usually Christmas Eve, which really made it seem like a special time. My father did his best to raise his kids and take care of a family, and it wasn't easy. But I have a lot of good memories, especially holiday memories.

I was fortunate to be surrounded by family. We lived on a farm, and my father's three youngest brothers lived right there on the farm with us because their father had passed away and there was nobody left to take care of the kids. My father accepted the responsibility. He took care of his mother and his three younger brothers, along with his own wife and five children. And my aunts lived nearby, too. So Christmas was a very happy and special time. Mother would pop popcorn and string it to decorate the tree. We always had a tree because there were some cedars growing on the farm, and each year Daddy would cut one down, put it by the fireplace and we'd all sit around and sing.

There would be at least twenty-five or thirty of us together on Christmas Eve and Christmas Day. All the kids got to play together, which was fun, and my mother, who was a great cook, always made sure we had a tremendous dinner. Most everybody had baked turkey, of course, but we did things a little different. Daddy and Uncle Harvey would go out and kill a turkey or two or three, and Mother would take that bird and fry it. We didn't bake the turkey, probably because we didn't have an oven big enough to bake it in. Instead, she'd cut it up and fry the breasts. And she'd take the dark meat from the legs and thighs and put it in the dressing. We'd take wild ducks out of a near-

Jim Ed Brown with sisters Maxine and Bonnie

by creek, too, and make duck dressing. The food was just fantastic. We'd sit around and eat until we could eat no more, and then everyone would leave for a few hours and come back later and eat some more.

Looking back, I know that we were poor, but it was all relative. We knew nothing about the rest of the world. We didn't have television. We didn't even have electricity. We had coal-oil lanterns, things like that. So we never felt deprived. Most of the time we didn't get much of anything for Christmas. If we did get a present, it was something that Mother and Daddy would make for us. I remember one year my daddy took a shingle off the house and made me a bean shooter; back then the rubber you found in inner tubes was real good rubber, so you could do that. A lot of years we didn't get anything. Sometimes we'd get some nuts or oranges, things like that. I was twelve years old before I got a store-bought present. It was a little watch — probably didn't cost but fifty cents. But, boy, was that watch special to me. I hadn't asked for it and I don't know how or why my parents gave it to me, but they did. And I thought it was just the most wonderful present a kid could get. I remember thinking, Wow! Now I can tell time! I don't recall any of the other store-bought presents I received over the years. I'm sure there were a few, but none of them stick out. I guess that one was special because it was the first.

Jim Ed Brown

15

ROY
Clark

ONE OF THE most versatile and successful entertainers in country music history, Roy Linwood Clark was born in Meherrin, Virginia, and grew up in Washington, D.C. His father was a computer programmer by vocation and a musician by avocation. Competent on most stringed instruments, Roy's father supplemented his income by playing at local dances. By the time he was fourteen, Roy was playing banjo, mandolin and guitar alongside his father. At sixteen he won a national competition for his banjo playing.

Roy traded his banjo and guitar for boxing gloves in his late teens and actually supported himself for a time as a light heavyweight in the professional ranks. Eventually, though, he realized that while it wouldn't be easy to carve out a living as a musician, it would surely be less painful than being a professional fighter. Roy's skill with a guitar allowed him to find steady work on the club circuit, and he soon developed a knack for connecting with audiences through a combination of music and humor. This led to radio and television appearances, and in the late 1950s he succeeded Jimmy Dean as host of the show *Country Style*. In the mid-1960s Roy made a successful guest appearance on the hit television comedy *The Beverly Hillbillies,* playing the sort of hokey but charming character that would become his trademark in later years. In 1963 he signed a contract with Capitol Records, and soon his career was in full flight.

Roy's first hit single was a cover of Bill Anderson's "The Tips of My Fingers." He had some of his biggest successes in the 1960s with the crossover hits "Yesterday When I Was Young" and "September Song." But it was as the cohost of the long-running television variety show *Hee Haw* that Roy gained worldwide recognition as a master comedian and musician. *Hee Haw* debuted on CBS in 1969 and was canceled just two years later. But it went on to achieve tremendous popularity in syndication, so much so that it ran for more than two decades. Along the way, Roy maintained a busy schedule of touring and recording. His hits in the 1970s included "Thank God and Greyhound You're Gone," "Come Live With Me," "Riders in the Sky" and "Somewhere Between Love and Tomorrow."

Roy went on to become one of the first country music stars to headline his own show on the Las Vegas strip. He also played to sellout crowds in the Soviet Union as part of a goodwill tour in 1976. Roy has won more than twenty-five awards in his career, including Country Music Association Entertainer of the Year in 1973, and a Grammy Award for his recording of "Alabama Jubilee" in 1982. He became a member of the Grand Ole Opry on August 22, 1987.

Roy
Remembers . . .

Everything changed for me the Christmas of my thirteenth year. That fall, a neighbor had let me strum on his Harmony arch-top guitar. It was the first time I'd ever played an instrument with six strings, from a treble to a bass. It was so different from the banjo and mandolin, and I was instantly hooked.

I got hold of a Sears catalog and circled the guitar I really liked, putting out less-than-subtle hints to my folks. I thought Christmas would never arrive! When it finally did, I was up before the crack of dawn and down the stairs in a flash. It was there, that Sears guitar, along with a copy of Smith's Three Hundred Chords for Guitar.

I'm sure I got lots of great stuff that year, but I have no idea what. The first moment I could, I grabbed that guitar and the book and ran up to my room. I played it all day, until my fingertips swelled. I had to put them in ice water. I was so consumed by learning to play that I would get up in the middle of the night and practice. Two weeks after Christmas, I'd gotten good enough to play a local dance with my dad. And that passion has never faded.

Roy on stage with Roy Acuff

Roy Clark

19

JOHN
Conlee

❦ ❦

THE AUTHOR AND voice behind the No. 1 hit "Common Man," John
Conlee is an unpretentious artist whose work comes directly from the
heart. He grew up in Kentucky and spent much of his boyhood working
on the family farm. Even then he had an interest in music, as evidenced by his role as a
tenor in the town's barbershop chorus. But it would take some time for John to realize
his dream of becoming a country music star.

He worked for a time as an embalmer at a funeral home, and later moved to
Nashville and took a job as a disc jockey. In the mid-1970s he got his break and signed
a contract with ABC/Dot Records (later acquired by MCA). He soon released his first

single, "Backside of Thirty." That song helped John earn the respect and admiration of critics and a handful of fans, but it wasn't until the release of "Rose Colored Glasses" in 1978 that his career began to soar. "Lady Lay Down" went to No. 1, as did a reissue of "Backside of Thirty." "Baby, You're Something" and "Before My Time," also released that year, helped John win the Academy of Country Music's Best New Male Vocalist award in 1979.

John was inducted into the Grand Ole Opry on February 7, 1981. He had his greatest chart success in 1983 and 1984 with the No. 1 hits "I'm Only in It for the Love," "As Long As I'm Rockin' With You," "In My Eyes" and "Common Man." Another single, the Dobie Gray–penned "Got My Heart Set on You," reached No. 1 in 1986.

John has received numerous awards and nominations over the course of his career, but his legacy includes more than music. Like the ordinary people who populate his songs, John is a man of simple tastes. He likes to spend as much time as possible on his family farm near Nashville, and devotes considerable time and energy to philanthropic causes, most notably on behalf of American farmers. John was instrumental in forming the Family Farm Defense Fund; along with John Mellencamp, Willie Nelson and Neil Young, he was one of the founders of Farm Aid, a series of benefit concerts that has raised millions of dollars.

John
Remembers . . .

I grew up in the 1950s in a small town in the middle of Kentucky. It was a time when most families lived in close proximity to each other. Consequently, there was much more interaction on a regular basis with grandparents and cousins than there is now for most families. Sunday dinner with grandparents was just a given in those days, and few weeks passed when it didn't occur. The Christmas season was a continuation of this family interaction, but in a bigger way.

Christmas Eve was when our family gathered for the BIG dinner, with as many family members as could be gathered up. And, of course, the part all of us kids enjoyed and looked forward to the most was the gift exchange that followed (after all the dishes were done).

The fifties were also the years when the Western was about the most popular form of entertainment—both in the movies and on television. No one was a bigger fan of them than me, and my favorite Christmas memory from those years placed me right in the middle of what I loved the most. It was the year that I received everything "cowboy." Included was a saddle and bridle (for the pony that was already in residence); a complete cowboy outfit, including hat, gloves, and chaps; AND . . . (this is the best part), any number of the current crop of cowboy cap guns, with enough caps to smoke up the whole house!

I have been blessed with many other meaningful Christmas seasons as the years have passed, but my "cowboy" Christmas will always be my favorite!

John Conlee

DIAMOND

Rio

Gene Johnson
Jimmy Olander
Brian Prout
Marty Roe
Dan Truman
Dana Williams

PERENNIAL CHART-TOPPER Diamond Rio was among the most successful country acts of the 1990s, but the band's musical roots can be traced back much farther. Lead singer Marty Roe, for example, was named after Marty Robbins and began singing at the age of three; bass player Dana Williams is a nephew of bluegrass kings and Grand Ole Opry members the Osborne Brothers; keyboard player Dan Truman studied classical piano at Brigham Young University; Jimmy Olander began playing banjo and guitar in his early teens; drummer

Brian Prout got his first kit for Christmas when he was eight years old; and Gene Johnson began playing the mandolin professionally before he reached high school.

Some members of the current lineup began playing together in the early 1980s as the Grizzly River Boys. By the time they were signed to Arista Records they had become the Tennessee River Boys, a band that first made its mark at Nashville's Opryland USA theme park. Urged by record company executives to change their name (the label felt the band would be mistaken for a gospel group), the Tennessee River Boys evolved into Diamond Rio (the name was taken from a pair of American truck manufacturers, Diamond T and Reo, which had merged to form Diamond-Reo). In 1991 the band released its self-titled debut album, *Diamond Rio*, which spawned the No. 1 hit single "Meet in the Middle." That same year the group also reached the Top 5 with the singles "Mirror, Mirror" and "Mama Don't Forget to Pray for Me." The album went platinum. In 1992, following the release of its second album, *Closer to the Edge*, the band was named Vocal Group of the Year by the Country Music Association.

Blending rich harmony vocals, solid bluegrass musicianship, and a rhythm section that often gives their music a rock 'n' roll flavor, Diamond Rio has earned a reputation as one of the most polished and professional groups in country music. In addition to being named Group of the Year a dozen times by country music associations and music industry publications, Diamond Rio has earned seven Grammy nominations and sold more than five million records worldwide. All of the band's studio albums have been certified either gold or platinum. Its No. 1 hits include "Norma Jean Riley," "In a Week or Two," "Love a Little Stronger," "Walkin' Away" and "How Your Love Makes Me Feel."

Diamond Rio first appeared on the Grand Ole Opry stage on October 4, 1991. On April 18, 1998, it became the first band since The Whites (some fourteen years earlier) to receive Opry membership.

Dana Williams
Remembers . . .

Fortunately, for me, I have been very blessed in that I've always been with family at Christmas. I know a lot of folks are separated at the holidays, but all of my life I have been surrounded by family at Christmastime. As a kid, growing up in Ohio, we were always together, and my grandparents were nearby. Now I live in Nashville, and I am probably in a radius of about six miles from all of my family and all of my wife's family. I really feel like that's a blessing, because I know a lot of people are out traveling, trying to get to one another's families. And that's appropriate, because Christmas is a time to come together.

Now I have a three-year-old son, and I'm going to do the best I can to make sure he knows Christmas should be a family thing. I think most people feel that way, but I just want it to be for him the way it was for me—not a painful thing to make happen.

It's funny: As our families have gotten older, Christmas has kind of grown. We're up to three days now. The night before Christmas Eve we'll go to my sister's house and everybody will gather up there and visit and be together. Then Christmas Eve we'll go to my wife's parents' house, and all the families will come over and we'll have a big Christmas dinner there. And then Christmas morning, of course, Santa Claus comes to my house, and my son gets up and opens his presents. Then later that day we'll go over to my parents' house and we'll all gather for another dinner. And then Christmas night, everybody comes back to our house. That's the way it ends. Everybody brings leftovers from the past two days and we try to get rid of everything. It's like, "Hey, man, can you shovel any more in?" And we play a game called White Elephant. Everybody brings a gift—most are kind of funny and weird, but some are nice. That's the fun of it. We draw names and do a grab bag, and everybody has a good time.

I have never been on the road during Christmas. I've had a couple Thanksgivings where I've been traveling, but not Christmas. We, as a band, always make sure that our schedule is clear for that. We just will not work. My mom and dad were always home when I was a kid, and I want it to be the same way for my boy. It takes a lot of work to make that happen for the guys in the band because we're scattered all over the country, but it's important. We travel a lot during the year, but Christmas is a time to be home. It is so easy, with all the stuff going on, all the rushing around, all the traveling, to forget what Christmas is all about. I try to remind friends and family to not forget the real reason for Christmas. And I remind myself all the time.

Dana's
Favorite Christmas Music

My daddy was always a real fan of the orchestrated type of Christmas music. We had a Jackie Gleason orchestra collection, which he always loved. And that stuck with me, so I went and got the CDs of it. Between Jackie Gleason and Nat King Cole's Christmas album, I'm all set. I have to listen to those every year to get in the spirit of things.

I don't know that I can say I have a specific favorite Christmas song. Of course, one of the classics of all time is "Oh, Holy Night"; you gotta love that. And there is a Skip Ewing song I really like called "It Wasn't His Child," which I sing in church sometimes, and which Trisha Yearwood had on her Christmas album. I love the story of that song. It's just very nice.

LITTLE JIMMY
Dickens

STILL ONE OF the most popular members of the Grand Ole Opry cast more than a half century after his induction, Little Jimmy Dickens was the oldest of thirteen children born into a poor family in rural West Virginia. He was barely in his teens when he came to the realization that there had to be an easier and more enjoyable way to make a living than by mining coal. Jimmy began singing on a local radio station in Beckley, West Virginia. Success on the local level led to a series of jobs in Michigan, Indiana and Ohio, and in November 1948, with the help of a recommendation from Roy Acuff, he joined the cast of the Grand Ole Opry.

Jimmy's first single, "Take an Old Cold Tater," was released in 1949 and established his reputation as a performer with a unique sense of humor. It also led his close friend Hank Williams to give Jimmy the nickname "Tater." Jimmy released dozens of hits on Columbia Records, including "Out Behind the Barn," "I'm Little, but I'm Loud," "Country Boy," "Wabash Cannonball" and "A-Sleepin' at the Foot of the Bed."

In the early 1960s Jimmy turned his attention to overseas ventures. He's made more than a dozen trips to Europe and has also toured Southeast Asia. A tireless performer, Jimmy, in 1964, became the first country artist to circle the globe on a world tour. In 1965 he achieved huge crossover success with his recording of the pop novelty song, "May the Bird of Paradise Fly Up Your Nose." More hits followed, including "Raggedy Ann" and "Preacher Man."

Jimmy experienced one of the highlights of his career in 1983, when he was inducted into the Country Music Hall of Fame. As testament to his enduring popularity, in 1989 Rounder Records released a collection of Jimmy's greatest hits. Although he's only four-feet, eleven-inches tall, Little Jimmy Dickens's reputation grows with each passing year, which probably explains why his friends in Nashville often refer to him as "Tater—The Littlest, but the Biggest Star at the Opry."

The Grand Ole Opry Country Christmas Album

Jimmy
Remembers . . .

I have many, many wonderful Christmas memories from my childhood, growing up in the Appalachian Mountains in West Virginia, in the coal-mining region. We were very poor, but we didn't know it. We thought the whole world lived the way we lived. Christmastime was special. We didn't get much—an orange, an apple, maybe a popcorn ball . . . and now and then a flashlight or something small. But I don't remember being unhappy or disappointed or anything like that. I remember the family. And the cooking . . . the meals my grandmother made over a woodstove. The smell of the pies she baked, the turkey. That's what I remember from my childhood Christmases. All good memories.

Then, of course, down through the years, I have other memories, good memories in a very different way. From 1960 to 1965, I spent a lot of time on the road. And I spent a lot of time with the American military during the holidays. I toured Vietnam three times, and Okinawa three times. Those Christmases I shall never forget, because of the appreciation the troops showed, the thanks they expressed for what we were doing.

One Christmas Eve stands out among all the others. I was playing in this old hotel in Saigon, which was occupied by the American military. I was doing the mess hall during the day and the club at night. Late on Christmas Eve, I was doing my show, and at about quarter to eleven, the sergeant came on the stage and stopped my performance, and said, very seriously, "We have to secure the club momentarily." So we all left the building. Well, it turned out that someone had spotted a suspicious-looking wire coming down out of the ceiling behind the refrigerator. And when they looked behind the refrigerator, they found fifty pounds of plastic explosives. It was a bomb! And there was

Little Jimmy Dickens

a detonator on the roof set to go off at midnight. On Christmas Eve! Now that was kind of a shaky deal. But they went up and defused it and everything was all right. The show was stopped and everyone came back inside and sat down together and drank and ate food and so forth, and laughed a little. We were all just happy to be alive. It was scary. It made me realize what a dangerous place it was, even though most people in the United States at the time really had no idea what was going on over there.

The next day I did another show at a club about thirty miles from Saigon, and it went smoothly. The crowd was wonderful. I'll tell you, there's nothing like performing for the military. They appreciated it so very much, because they got so little entertainment in Vietnam. And just imagine—to be that far away from your loved ones and your family on Christmas Day. When someone came to entertain them, boy, they were an appreciative audience. They really wouldn't let you off the stage. The reception was unbelievable. It was hard being thousands of miles from home at Christmastime, but they made the best of it. Everybody was jolly and having fun. If anything, they were a little rowdier than most people at Christmas. I think that's understandable.

Jimmy's
Favorite Christmas Carol

I love all Christmas music, I really do. But if I had to pick a favorite song, it would be "Oh, Holy Night." I don't know why . . . it just does something for me. I love to sing that song, and I love to hear it.

HOLLY
Dunn

A GIFTED SONGWRITER AND singer, Holly Dunn grew up in San Antonio, Texas, in a home where music and creativity were warmly embraced. She was just a toddler when she made her first visit to the San Antonio Municipal Auditorium to see a performance by a group of stars from the Grand Ole Opry, and before long she was singing songs and playing the guitar.

Holly's older brother Chris moved to Nashville to begin a songwriting career while Holly was still in college. His success inspired Holly, and after graduating from Abilene Christian University with a degree in public relations and advertising, she followed suit. Within a year she had landed her first writing contract. Holly spent the early part of the 1980s establishing a reputation as one of the finest songwriters in Nashville, penning hits for Louise Mandrell, Christy Lane and The Whites, among others.

In 1986 Holly began recording her own material, and she quickly built a large and loyal following. She was named Top New Female Vocalist by the Academy of Country Music in 1986, the same year her version of "Daddy's Hands" landed in the Top 10 and received two Grammy nominations. Holly had written the song as a Father's Day gift for her dad in 1985, and it was recorded by The Whites. In 1987 she won the Country Music Association's Horizon Award, and in 1988 she won the BMI Country Songwriter of the Year award.

Holly had a string of No. 1 hits in the late 1980s, including "Are You Ever Gonna Love Me," "Love Someone Like Me" and "You Really Had Me Going." Having already made numerous appearances on the Opry stage, she was invited to join the cast on October 14, 1989.

After taking a three-year break from recording in the early 1990s, Holly released a new album, *Life and Love and All the Stages,* in 1995. In 1997 she became the popular drive-time disc jockey on Detroit's WWWW-FM.

Holly
Remembers . . .

I have three older brothers, so Christmas at our house was always very noisy, full of life. My father collected those Firestone albums of Christmas music, and he'd put a stack of them on the turntable and we'd play them until they all dropped. Then we'd flip the whole stack over and run through them again. We always decorated our tree well before Christmas. Some families, I know, decorate on Christmas Eve, but we always had it decorated before that. We did the tradition of waking up on Christmas morning and opening up presents. It was kind of like a gift orgy. And it was always fun to try to guess what you were going to get. Sometimes we'd sit around and sing a little bit, pick a little bit, but mostly we were just there together as family, laughing a lot, telling a lot of jokes about each other. My father was a Church of Christ minister and my mom is a landscape artist, so I grew up in a real rich home as far as art, culture, music and literature. It was wonderful. But the best part is that we all have a good sense of humor and enjoy being together.

I grew up in San Antonio, and of course there's a heavy Mexican-American influence down there that flavors everything—in the same way that the Cajun culture flavors New Orleans. So instead of the usual Christmas dinner of turkey and ham and all the traditional trimmings that you typically think of, we always had Mexican food. Dad would go down to this little tamale factory and he would get several dozen tamales, and Mom would make up a big old thing of chicken enchiladas and a big pot of pinto beans. We'd have the basic big, greasy, delicious Mexican meal. And we'd eat until we had to just lay around and recover. We still do this, actually. It's gone on for decades. We get

Holly Dunn

together at Mom's house and we still have what we call the Dunn *tamalada*, which is, I believe, Spanish for "big party . . . big blowout." We have enchiladas, tamales, beans, the whole nine yards. And we all really look forward to it. We save up our fat grams from the whole year just for this meal. I love traditions. I love Christmas. I love decorating. Once I owned my own home it was fun to fix it up for Christmas, and yet I still have a very Southwestern theme going—chili pepper lights on the tree, things like that. My house is decorated year-round pretty Southwestern, so I carry that influence with me.

I've only missed one Christmas at home in my entire life, and that was 1979, my first year in Nashville. I had moved at the end of August, so by Christmas I was still brand-new in town, and I had no money at all. I couldn't afford to go home. I lived in a little second-floor apartment, and I had this pitiful little Charlie Brown Christmas tree. My folks sent me a care package of goodies—presents and some other things—just so I'd have something under my tree. But I was totally alone. My brother lived here, too, but he and his wife had gone out of town to be with her folks, so I had nobody with whom I could spend Christmas. I remember feeling very sorry for myself. I unwrapped my little gifts and cried. I listened to some Christmas songs and got totally depressed. I was just so miserable and lonely, and I swore that day that I would never, ever miss another Christmas with my family. And I never have. The next year I made it back, and I've made it back every year since. That lonely Christmas in Nashville really brought home to me the importance of being with people you love, especially at the holidays. I just never wanted to be away from my family after that. And even as busy as I've been on the road, through the years, I've always managed to get back home.

One Christmas I will always remember was 1996, the year before my father died. He had been ill for a while, and although I'd usually been so busy touring, trying to be a "star," that I'd just sort of blow in for a couple days at Christmas, this time I was determined to take about ten days and just go home. And I did. I went home and spent ten days with my mom and dad, like I hadn't done since I left home really. It was a real blessing to be with them, and to bond, and to be just their daughter again, and not a country music singer.

Holly Dunn

BILLY
Grammer

Agrand Old Opry cast member since February 27, 1959, Billy Grammer is a versatile musician who rose from the humblest of backgrounds to the top of the country music charts. The son of an Illinois coal miner and farmer, he was one of thirteen children. Billy was an easygoing but confident kid who aspired to big things. Music was not his first choice as a ticket to a better life; education was. Billy wanted to go to college and get a degree in engineering. But after falling in love with the guitar, he charted another course.

Billy served a brief stint in the U.S. Army and later worked as an apprentice toolmaker. An audition with Connie B. Gay, a Virginia disc jockey who was promoting

Grand Ole Opry acts in the region, proved to be Billy's first big break in the music business. While riding high on the success of his biggest single, "Gotta Travel On," Billy was invited to join the cast of the Grand Ole Opry. The song sold more than a million copies and was a hit with both country and pop audiences.

Although he never matched the success of "Gotta Travel On," Billy remained a popular performer on the Opry and was always in demand as a session guitar player. A true guitar connoisseur, he eventually focused his attention on the manufacturing end of the music business. It was Billy's goal to produce the finest flat-top guitar on the market. Whether he succeeded or not, of course, is largely a matter of taste. But reviews for the early Grammer guitars, which appeared in 1965, were universally favorable. In fact, the very first Grammer guitar has a permanent home in the Grand Ole Opry Museum.

Billy

Remembers . . .

I was raised a farm boy in southern Illinois, and we didn't even have electricity until 1941. I'm from a real big family. My mother birthed thirteen children. I'm the oldest. I've got eight brothers and four sisters. How would you do that today? There's no way. But we grew our own vegetables, we had a garden, raised everything. I had three pair of overalls—one relatively new when school was starting, one that was starting to fade and one totally faded that I used for the barn work. That was enough.

My dad was a coal miner, and my mother took care of the family. At the time of this story, there were seven kids in the family. And we scrubbed all of our clothes on a washboard in a washtub. I think the happiest Christmas probably that I ever had was when Dad got my mother a gasoline engine–operated washing machine. Scrubbing for seven kids was exhausting. Of course, we helped her—we were raised that way, disciplined that way—but my mother did most of the work. So this was a great present for her.

It wasn't the easiest thing to do, either, to hide it from her. You don't just put a washing machine under the tree. Dad had it hidden in the barn. He slipped it in there one day, had it hauled in, crated, and kept it there. My mom never went in the barn. We went in there . . . the kids. We gathered the eggs, milked the cow, fed the hogs and all that stuff. So I knew it was out there. Some of the other kids didn't. They knew something was out there in a box, but they weren't sure what it was. Then, on Christmas morning, Dad took the washing machine out of the crate and brought it to the back of the house. He put ribbons on it, and a sign saying "Merry Christmas" and all that stuff. It was beautiful. And I remember my mom's reaction. The first thing she said was, "Well, Arch, it looks very nice, but I don't know how to operate it."

Billy Grammer

Funny thing, though, it didn't save a lot of time. Usually you did a half day's work trying to get the dad-gum thing started. It was like the old kick start on a motorcycle. It was a Briggs and Stratton engine, which is one of the best now, but at that time . . . well, the carburetion and everything was a little less sophisticated than it is now. You'd go through a whole process to get the machine running: kick, kick . . . choke, choke . . . overchoke . . . flooded . . . wait . . . try again. I guarantee you there were many times we spent over an hour kicking that thing and trying to get it started.

That same year, I was twelve years old, and my dad got me my first gun. I had accompanied him hunting many times, and I knew all the safety standards. So I was ready. But I wasn't expecting anything. Like I said, we didn't have much money. But Dad got me a .22 rifle, a little Winchester bolt-action model 67. How my father managed that, I'm not sure. He just outdid himself. I know he had good credit. When it came payday, if he owed any money, he'd make the rounds in that old Model A car of his, and he'd pay a dollar here, a dollar there. People trusted him, and when he needed something, he got it. He never would overbuy. He didn't dream and buy; he bought necessities, and my mom needed that washer. But every year at Christmas, somehow, Dad always bought us little presents. There was always something under the tree. I got a harmonica one year, a knife another year. But we never expected big things. So when I got this rifle, which must have cost $9.95, I was shocked, because that was an awful lot of money back then.

I guess I had a double Christmas that year, you know? Mom got a washing machine, and I got a rifle.

GEORGE
Hamilton IV

THE PROLIFIC GEORGE HAMILTON IV grew up in Winston-Salem, North Carolina. He began his career as a pop music star, riding such hits as "High School Romance," "A Rose and a Baby Ruth" and "Why Don't They Understand" to the top of the charts in the late 1950s. But that was merely the first incarnation of an artist who would eventually evolve into an international folk superstar.

George moved to Nashville in 1959 and made a smooth transition from pop to country with a string of hits, including "Before This Day Ends," "If You Don't Know I Ain't Gonna Tell You," "Truck Driving Man" and "Abilene," a 1963 classic that remains his biggest seller. Along the way George became a regular performer on the Grand Ole Opry, and was invited to join the cast in 1960.

Never one to settle for comfort, George began exploring new musical and geographic territories in the late 1960s and early 1970s. During an appearance at the Horseshoe Tavern in Toronto, he met acclaimed Canadian singer-songwriter Gordon Lightfoot. Soon, George was recording and performing material by Lightfoot and other Canadian folksingers such as Joni Mitchell, Ian Tyson, Buffy Saint-Marie and Leonard Cohen. Once he embraced the folk music scene, George began pushing the boundaries of his own career. He appeared at the first International Festival of Country Music in Wembley, England, in 1969. He also became the first U.S. country singer to perform in Russia and Czechoslovakia. Solidifying his reputation as a truly international performer, George became the first American country artist to host his own television series in Great Britain.

George's hectic travel schedule prompted him to leave the Opry in 1971 and establish a base of operations in his hometown of Winston-Salem. Five years later, though, he rejoined the Opry. Today George lives in Nashville and continues to maintain a heavy international touring schedule.

George
Remembers . . .

My favorite memories of Christmas are church-related. My father was a Sunday school superintendent at Fries Memorial Moravian Church in Winston-Salem. And my mother was the kind of woman who made sure we were in church every time the doors opened. It was the center of our social life: youth fellowship, Boy Scouts, youth choir, Sunday school, Bible study. Church was everything to us, especially at Christmastime.

The Moravian church is the first and oldest organized international Protestant church. It's a pre-Reformation church founded in 1457 in Moravia and Bohemia, in part of what is now the Czech Republic. These people were the first to send missionaries to the New World, and they had a great influence on the Wesley brothers—John Wesley and Charles Wesley met up with some Moravian missionaries on a boat to Georgia, back in 1735, I believe.

On Christmas Eve in the Moravian Church, we gather for what we call the Christmas Eve Love Feast. It's a beautiful service, a worship service signifying brotherly love, while sharing a simple meal: a mug of coffee and a slightly sweetened bun. Basically, it's celebrated in the spirit of the Agape meal. In the early days of the Christian Church, people gathered together to express their love for the Lord and for each other around the dinner table. This was before there were formal church buildings. A lot of Christians met in private homes around the table, as did Jesus, who issued many of his most important pronouncements around the meal.

So, for this particular service we all gather and sing carols. It's not a communion service—it's a fellowship meal. A very simple, symbolic thing. We gather in the church and the ladies of the church come down the aisle carrying trays of these sweetened buns. And they're dressed in traditional Moravian costumes from several hundred years ago. Then the men of the church come down the aisles carrying coffee. And we pass the buns and coffee out to everybody. We sing carols, and then the minister speaks briefly about how Jesus came into a dark world at a time, much like today, when there was a lot of trouble and sadness. He came to bring light into a dark world. And at that point the ladies and gentlemen who are serving everybody—they're called "dieners"—they come down the aisle with lighted candles, which they distribute to the congregation. The church lights go out and everybody receives a little beeswax candle trimmed with red ribbons. The ribbon symbolizes the sacrifice of Christ, the blood of Christ, who died for all of us. And the flame is the flame of love, which he came to kindle in the hearts of men and women. The message of that, of course, is that this flame of love will burn forever, to His joy and to our salvation. And the minister alludes to that, how if we each just lit our own little candle in our little corner of the world, if we tried to reach out to others in Christian love, what a bright world it would be. Then he asks us to raise our candles high, and as we do, the whole church is filled with light. It's illuminated with beautiful candlelight. Then there's a short benediction, and we all go out into the darkness of the night, carrying our little lighted candles, symbolic of going out into the world with a flame of love.

The Christmas Eve Love Feast is a time when families come together. It's a magical evening anyway. It's Christmas, which is a favorite time of year for a lot of people. And the fact that we gathered for so many years at this service, in this church, and sang carols . . . it was a binding and bonding sort of thing. When people pass away, memories of them come back every year with this service. It's a sweet, poignant celebration of Christmas, and it brings back memories of all the years past when your parents were still living and you were a little kid at Christmastime. I guess the special joy of it is to see the excitement and wonder in the eyes of the little children. You know that in the back of their minds they're anxious to get home and get to sleep and wait for Santa Claus, but that's all right. That's part of the magic for children.

The very special thing about the Christmas Eve Love Feast service is that it takes me back. You know that phrase, "We all become little children at Christmastime"? Well, I find myself feeling like a child again, just as excited as ever. It's something I've been through so many times, but it's like a Christmas tree: It's evergreen. It's timeless. I was thinking the other day as I was touring around the countryside, listening to carols, how timeless some of them are. It's the same way with this service. There's not a single Moravian church in Tennessee, so we usually go back to Winston-Salem. That's where my wife is from, too. And when I step into that church, it takes me right back to my childhood.

George with his son, George Hamilton V

George's
Favorite Christmas Carol

There's an old Moravian Christmas carol called "Morning Star" that I just love. It's several hundred years old, and it comes from the old country. It's in the Moravian hymnal:

Morning Star, O cheering sight!

Ere Thou cam'st how dark earth's night!

Morning Star, O cheering sight!

Ere Thou cam'st how dark earth's night!

Jesus mine, in me shine;

In me shine, Jesus mine;

Fill my heart with light divine.

Morning Star, Thy glory bright!

Far excels the sun's clear light.

Morning Star, Thy glory bright!

Far excels the sun's clear light.

Jesus be, constantly,

Constantly, Jesus be

More than thousand suns to me.

Thy glad beams, Thou Morning Star

Cheer the nations near and far.

Thy glad beams, Thou Morning Star

Cheer the nations near and far.

Thee we own, Lord alone,

Lord alone, Thee we own

Man's great savior, God's dear Son.

Morning Star, my soul's true Light,

Tarry not, dispel my night;

Morning Star, my soul's true Light,

Tarry not, dispel my night;

Jesus mine, in me shine;

In me shine, Jesus mine;

Fill my heart with light divine.

George Hamilton IV

STONEWALL
Jackson

IN NEARLY A half century of singing and writing music, Stonewall Jackson has produced an immense body of work: ten gold singles, five gold albums, and more than fifty singles in the Top 10! An extraordinary achievement, by any measure, but particularly impressive when you consider Stonewall's background.

First of all, yes, that is his real name. The youngest of three children, he was born in Tabor City, North Carolina. He never really got to know his father, who died when Stonewall was only two years old. With no money and no job prospects in the region, Stonewall's mother packed up her children and hitchhiked to Georgia, where she helped out on her brother's farm. When Stonewall was sixteen he altered his birth certificate and enlisted in the U.S. Army. When the Army discovered Stonewall was underage, he was discharged. One year later he joined the Navy, and it was while serving in that branch of the armed forces that he learned how to play the guitar.

After another stint on the farm, during which he saved enough money to buy a new pickup truck, Stonewall drove to Nashville in 1954 to begin what he hoped would be a new career: music. His break came in the form of an audition for Wesley Rose of Acuff-Rose Publishing. By November 1956 Stonewall, although still a virtual unknown, was a member of the Grand Ole Opry roster. The Opry invitation turned out to be prescient, though, for Stonewall went on to become one of the most prolific and popular artists in country music. His first No. 1 hit, in 1959, was "Life to Go." "Waterloo," released in 1960, hit Top 10 on both the country and pop charts. For the better part of the next two decades, Stonewall released one hit record after another, including the Top 10 hits "Why I'm Walkin'," "A Wound Time Can't Erase," "Old Showboat" and "Don't Be Angry."

Stonewall celebrated forty years with the Opry in November 1996. On July 25, 1997, he was presented with the fourth annual Ernest Tubb Memorial Award for his outstanding contributions to the country music industry.

Stonewall

Remembers . . .

B*ack in the winter of 1965, when my son was about five years old, I got this crazy idea that it would be great to get him a pony for Christmas. His name is Stonewall Junior, but everyone calls him "Terp," like a little land terrapin, a little turtle, because when he was first born he used to flip over on his stomach and he'd wear the knees and elbows off his clothes squirming around. Anyway, for a Christmas present I decided to get him a Shetland pony. Now, they call them ponies, and people think of them as being small, but the truth is they're about half the size of a real horse, which is still pretty big. We had the whole thing set up where Santa Claus would come to our house while the boy's mother would have him over at his grandparents' house. That way, when he came home, he'd think that Santa Claus brought the horse. So here in my music room I put down a big piece of plywood, a big old rug and all that to protect the floor, and I put that horse on it and tied him up to the wall—right there inside the house—so when Terp came in with his mother, his eyes bugged plumb out. He was knocked out, boy. So we led him around out there in the yard all day, with him on the horse, and he was having a great big ball with it. And then, about an hour later, he got to wanting to take it over to his grandparents' place, which was about six miles away, to show it off, you know? He was so proud of that horse.*

Now, you have to remember that me and my wife were pretty young back then, so we were still kind of green when it came to being parents. I say that because we need some kind of excuse for what happened so people don't think we were just plain ignorant. You see, I had just bought a brand-new Cadillac that fall, and the only way we could get the pony over to Terp's grandparents' place was to put him in the back of the car. So that's what we did. We put a Shetland pony in the backseat of a Cadillac. My wife sat in the front with Terp and our baby-sitter. Well, of course, that pony got to feeling a little tight back there and pretty soon he got to carrying on and jumping and whatnot, and he kicked the door off that Cadillac! So they stopped the car and got the horse out and walked it along the side of the road. My wife was holding Terp's hand and the baby-sitter was leading the pony.

Now, you have to understand that I try to like everybody, but unfortunately I have to admit that there are some strange people out there, even on Christmas Day, and a few of them drove by my wife and son and threw a pack of firecrackers at them. Well, naturally, the horse had a fit, and it was all they could do to keep him under control. Eventually they walked him over to the side of the road and got him calmed down. Terp got to show the pony to his granddaddy, and everybody lived happily ever after. It's kind of funny, though, isn't it? Putting a horse in the back of a Cadillac? I think that's a good Christmas story.

The Grand Ole Opry Country Christmas Album

Jim & Jesse

Jim McReynolds
Jesse McReynolds

F OR MORE THAN half a century brothers Jim and Jesse McReynolds have been entertaining audiences with their sweet vocal harmonies and bluegrass brilliance. Raised in the mountains of southwest Virginia in a family of farmers and coal miners, Jim and Jesse were fortunate to be surrounded by relatives who loved playing and listening to traditional "mountain music." Their grandfather Charles was a fiddler who played with a local band at the turn of the century and later landed a recording deal with RCA; their father, Claude, played fiddle in Charles's band; and their mother, Savannah, was a gospel singer.

By the time they were in their early teens, Jim and Jesse were already accomplished musicians, Jim on guitar and Jesse on mandolin. So adept was Jesse that he developed a stunningly nimble style of playing known as "cross-picking" (or, more affectionately, "McReynolds") that helped give the brothers a truly distinctive sound.

Under the name Jim & Jesse and the Virginia Boys (their backup band included a banjo and fiddle), the brothers signed their first recording contract in 1952, with Capitol Records, and released their first hit single, "The Flame of Love." Over the years they have also recorded with Columbia, Epic, Rounder, Opryland and their own label, Old Dominion Records. Jim & Jesse's most popular songs include "Diesel on My Tail," "Paradise," "I Wish You Knew," "Are You Missing Me?" and "Cotton Mill Man."

Tireless performers known for their integrity as well as their incomparable musicianship, Jim & Jesse have been members of the Grand Ole Opry cast since March 2, 1964. They have been honored with a star in the Country Music Hall of Fame's Walkway of Stars and induction into Bill Monroe's Bluegrass Hall of Fame. On September 23, 1997, at a ceremony at the White House, First Lady Hillary Rodham Clinton honored Jim & Jesse with the National Heritage Fellowship Award from the National Endowment for the Arts.

Jesse

Remembers . . .

One of my most memorable Christmases was in the year of 1943, when I was fourteen years old. It started the day after Thanksgiving, when my brother Jim and I were out riding in a car with a couple of friends. While trying to avoid a dog that had wandered out into the road, the driver lost control of the car. We flew off the road, rolled down an embankment and flipped over several times. All four doors of the car were ripped off. I wound up under part of a seat, with the driver lying on top of me. At first, I didn't know if I was alive or dead. I pulled myself out of the car and didn't feel any pain. I thought I had escaped injury, until I got up to take my first step. My left foot looked a little out of place, and when I went to put my foot down, I was horrified to see my leg bone sticking right into the dirt. The only thing holding my foot on to my leg were a few ligaments.

No one else seemed to be hurt, except for cuts and bruises. I ended up in the hospital with a leg mangled so severely that the doctor had to confer with my parents about whether to amputate my foot or try to save it. Thanks to a new drug called penicillin, which was used to fight infection, they decided to try to save my foot. I was hospitalized for twenty-six days, and since I could move my toes a little, I was lucky enough to go home a few days before Christmas.

The weather was very cold the day they took me home, and since we lived up in the mountains, we could only get a car within about a half mile of the house. I remember my brother meeting us down at the main road with a horse and sled to take me up and around the mountain lane to our house. My dog Shep was with him, and he was just *so happy to see me after my being away for a month. Shep was the best dog I ever had. He stayed close by my side all the way home, running along by the sled.*

Wrapped in lots of blankets to ward off the cold, I was carried into the house, where it was nice and warm. The coal-burning stove was in the bedroom, where I would have to stay for Christmas . . . and a long time afterward. Many of my friends and relatives came to visit me at Christmas that year. I remember getting more presents than usual. But I sure missed going out rabbit hunting with Shep.

My uncles would come by on weekends, and we'd play music. I really enjoyed that. During the week I'd have lots of time to practice on the mandolin and fiddle. It must have driven my mom crazy, listening to me learning to play fiddle day after day, but she never complained.

It was almost a year before I could walk again. But I knew by then, after listening to the Grand Ole Opry every Saturday night, and practicing every chance I got, that playing music was what I always wanted to do. So I can say that the greatest gift I ever got for Christmas was to have two feet to walk on. And I just thank the Lord for taking a tragic thing like an auto accident (and a badly broken leg) and making something good of it. Like fifty-two years of entertaining people and being lucky enough to be a member of the world's greatest country music show, the Grand Ole Opry.

$\mathcal{J}im$

Remembers . . .

We grew up in the coal-mining region of Wise County, Virginia, and lived on a hillside farm. There was always a lot of work to be done, and about the only time we would go to town would be on a Saturday. Christmas was quite different from the ones we experience today. It didn't take long to do our Christmas shopping, because there wasn't a lot of money to spare.

The one thing that we looked forward to most was our mother's Christmas dinner, which consisted of fried chicken, fried or creamed potatoes, green beans, corn and other vegetables, which were all homegrown (including the chicken). And she always baked an old-fashioned Molasses Stack Cake, which was our favorite.

Living in coal-mining country and being farmers, too, our dad always kept dynamite around to blow out stumps to help clear the land. We learned how to use it at a very early age, and Dad always had to restock after the holidays. We never had too many complaints about shooting the dynamite, except one Christmas when a bunch of the neighborhood boys got together and thought of a way to create excitement. We decided we would get everyone's attention, so we took sixty sticks to the top of a mountain and set off a large blast!

There sure was a lot of talk about our fireworks, and all the neighbors were trying to figure out what had happened. I don't think any of us ever admitted to setting off the blast, in fear of having to pay for the trees it knocked down. Once when we were blowing stumps with the dynamite, one of our dogs ate about half a stick, and later in the evening the dog chased our mule into the barn. The mule kicked the dog and blew the barn down! They both recovered, but every time we would have a bad thunderstorm, it would be days before we could find either of them. It seemed we always had exciting things happening on the farm.

Although times were hard and presents were few, Christmas was always a special time. We were taught the real meaning of Christmas, for our mother always read the Bible and taught us that God's greatest gift to man was His Son, Jesus Christ, the Savior.

THE
Judds

Naomi Judd
Wynonna Judd

O NE OF THE MORE improbable success stories in country music, the Judds began life as a striking mother-daughter combo who looked and acted more like sisters. They rose to prominence in the 1980s and eventually became the bestselling duo in country history.

Naomi Judd was born Diana Ellen Judd in Ashland, Kentucky. Before she had even graduated from high school, Naomi had married her high school sweetheart and given birth to a daughter, Wynonna. When Wynonna was four years old, the family moved to California, where Naomi had a second child, Ashley. Three years later, though, the marriage dissolved and Naomi eventually settled with her daughters in Kentucky. They lived an isolated life in a mountaintop house, with no telephone or television. Naomi supported her family in a variety of ways—as a secretary and model, among other things—and although they didn't have much money, they became extra-ordinarily close and supportive of one another.

To pass the time and entertain themselves, they often listened to the Grand Ole Opry radio show. Wynonna learned to play the guitar, and soon she was singing with her mother. In 1979 the family pulled up roots again, this time to pursue a dream in Nashville. Naomi took a job as a nurse while the girls attended school. At the same time, Naomi and Wynonna began performing live, most notably on Ralph Emery's morning television show. They shopped demo tapes cut on a cheap little recorder. Their näiveté, however, was outweighed by their talent. Listeners could tell that Wynonna had a brilliant and powerful voice, and that Naomi's songs had heart and intelligence. In March of 1983 their hard work and patience was rewarded with a contract from RCA Records.

The duo's first release, an EP titled *The Judds,* yielded a hit single, "Had a Dream." A full-length album, *Why Not Me?,* was released in 1984, and with that the Judds found enormous mainstream success. The singles "Mama He's Crazy" and "Why Not Me" both hit No.1, and the latter also was honored as Single of the Year in 1985 by the Country Music Association. By the end of 1985 they had released another album, *Rockin' With the Rhythm,* and had picked up a handful of major awards, including the Country Music Association's Horizon Award and a Grammy. They had two platinum albums to their credit and six No. 1 singles.

Three more hit albums followed—*Heartland* (1987), *Greatest Hits* (1988) and *Love Can Build a Bridge* (1990)—before Judds fans were stunned by the news that Naomi was suffering from hepatitis C. The illness sapped Naomi's strength and made it nearly impossible for her to withstand the rigors of touring, so in 1991 she announced her retirement. After a long and emotional farewell tour, The Judds disbanded and Wynonna embarked on a solo career. Although the transition was enormously difficult for Wynonna, she proved to be resilient. In 1992 she released her first solo album on MCA Records. In the years since she has remained one of the most successful and popular artists in country music, selling more than nine million records as a solo performer and placing more than a dozen singles in the *Billboard* Top 10.

In 1999, fans of the Judds were treated to a reunion concert by Naomi (whose disease is in remission) and Wynonna. They performed together at a New Year's

Eve show in Phoenix, in front of 11,000 fans. Wynonna's little sister, Ashley, who has gone on to become a star in Hollywood, served as emcee of the event. Naomi had kept busy in the intervening years through her work as a spokesperson for the American Liver Foundation, as an actress in made-for-television movies and as the author of a bestselling autobiography, but clearly she had missed performing with her daughter. So it shouldn't have come as a great surprise that after the New Year's concert, plans for an extended Judds tour were announced.

Naomi

Remembers . . .

(Taken from Naomi's autobiography, *Love Can Build a Bridge*, this story recalls Christmas of 1989, when Ashley Judd was a college student who had spent the fall semester studying at École des Beaux-Arts in Paris. Ashley was scheduled to return from Europe for the holidays on a Pan Am flight from Frankfurt, Germany, to New York, on the same day that Pan Am flight 103 exploded in the air over Lockerbie, Scotland.)

No one talked as twenty of us sat huddled together in the waiting area of the Nashville terminal watching the plane land. As the passengers began disembarking, it felt as if my head was going to explode from tension as I watched people appear one by one in the doorway. No Ashley. That day I had been reliving every event of Ashley's life. Suddenly, like some miraculous apparition, she appeared. A great cry went up from our group. We made instant eye contact through the flailing arms of the huddle, and she squealed, "Hi, Mommy!"

Ashley's flight had left Frankfurt twenty minutes after flight 103. The airline did its best to protect the passengers from learning of the tragedy. The phone lines were all jammed at the New York airport, and in an effort to take care of the grieving families, the connecting passengers arriving in La Guardia had been marched straight to their connecting flights without making any phone calls. Ashley later became distraught when she found out what happened, realizing that she'd slept in the same room with some of these students and eaten breakfast with them only hours before their tragic death.

It was the strangest holiday we've ever had. I couldn't have cared less whether we had a tree, a single present. All I did was hug and stare at Ashley. Wynonna couldn't let Ashley and me out of her sight. I was completely haunted by the crash of Pan Am flight 103. I'd awaken in the middle of the night, grieving for the parents, and creep into Ashley's room and sit on her bed till dawn watching her while she slept.

—FROM *Love Can Build a Bridge*, BY NAOMI JUDD AND BUD SCHAETZLE

HANK
Locklin

LAWRENCE HANKINS LOCKLIN was born in McLellan, Florida, and began teaching himself guitar while he was still in grammar school. A frequent competitor in local talent contests and a featured performer on radio station WCOA in Pensacola, he steadily refined his singing and guitar playing throughout his teenage years. After graduating from high school, Hank supported himself by working as a farmer and shipyard worker, but he never lost sight of his goal: to become a professional musician.

Hank recorded his first hit single, "The Same Sweet Girl," in 1949. Four years later he had his first No. 1 record, "Let Me Be the One," which led to a contract with RCA Victor and, finally, security. In 1957 Hank had a crossover hit with "Geisha Girl," which fared well on the pop charts as well. The same was true of "Send Me the Pillow You Dream On," released in 1958. His most popular record was "Please Help Me, I'm Falling," which, in 1960, spent half the year atop the country charts and was also a pop hit in the United States and the United Kingdom. That same year, on November 9, Hank was invited to join the Grand Ole Opry. His hits in the 1960s included "From Here to There to You," "Happy Journey," "One Step Ahead of My Time," "Followed Closely by My Teardrops" and "Happy Birthday to Me."

Hank has received numerous honors for his work over the years, including an ASCAP award for the album *Country Hall of Fame*, and *Cash Box* and *Juke Box* awards for "Please Help Me, I'm Falling." In addition to his success on these shores, Hank has enjoyed a rabid following in Ireland, where his tenor is one of the most popular country voices in history.

Hank with Carol Lee Cooper, 1999

$\mathcal{H}ank$
Remembers . . .

I must have been six or seven years old. In those days we lived out in the country, a little place called McLellan, in Florida, about three miles south of the Alabama border. We lived in a big house. And of course we had a fireplace for the heat. If I remember, I had the flu two or three times along about that time, and I must have been sleeping with my parents. It was Christmas morning, the middle of the night. I got up about four o'clock, it was still dark, and Mom and Dad had a big fire in the fireplace. I got up and, of course, you had a chamber then, you didn't have indoor plumbing or anything like that. So I got up and I sat down on the chamber pot, and I sort of looked around, in a sleepy haze, and I looked under the edge of the bed; I don't even know why. I don't think I was really expecting anything. But there was a little box, like a shoebox, and in that box there was an apple and an orange and a couple of hazelnuts. And a little whistle that you could blow, and if you hummed, you could hum a tune. And that was it. But it was magical. I still remember sitting on that chamber, and I can still see a little box under the bed, right next to me, and I remember how it looked, how everything was placed in the box, the apple and orange on each side, the whistle sorta in the middle, and the nuts on the ends. I wasn't supposed to see it until the next morning, of course, until we all got up. Now that was exciting.

There was another time I remember we went to someone's house, and they had a Christmas tree, and this guy dressed up like Santa Claus, and he came in through the door. I don't think I even got a present, we just happened to be visiting. But he gave out his presents off the tree, he cried out "Ho-ho-ho" and went out through the window. The windows back then were different—you just opened them up and used a stick to prop it up. I don't even think they had curtains. I thought it was magic, though—my first time seeing Santa Claus.

Music was a big part of Christmas, too. My dad started off as a fireman for the lumber company, on one of the trains that hauled the trees from McLellan to Milton, Florida, about thirty-five miles away. Then he had a thirty-acre farm, and we moved. He planted corn and cotton and beans, stuff like that. He worked very hard. But what he really liked to do was play the fiddle. I remember going to these frolics around Christmastime, big dances, with folks from all over the place. Usually the band wouldn't have a rhythm section, so the rhythm would be two broom straws about fifteen to eighteen inches long and probably close to an eighth of an inch around. So one person, while my dad was playing the fiddle, would take the two straws and make a rhythm, while he's playing, by hitting them against the strings. You could really hear it, too, because the place probably wasn't more than thirty feet in diameter and everyone was tucked in real tight. That was a lot of fun.

Hank's
Favorite Christmas Song

I like "Rudolph the Red-Nosed Reindeer." It's a great holiday song. I even recorded it once, back when Chet Atkins was my producer.

LORETTA

Lynn

THANKS TO HER bestselling autobiography, *Coal Miner's Daughter*, and a subsequent feature film of the same name, millions of people around the world know all about the story of Loretta Lynn. But it remains achingly poignant and, ultimately, uplifting.

Born Loretta Webb in the hills of eastern Kentucky, she was indeed the daughter of a coal miner. And her struggle to artistic success was every bit as dramatic as Hollywood would have you believe. A sickly child, Loretta didn't walk until she was four years old, and on three occasions nearly succumbed to illness. But she proved to be a girl of uncommon strength and will. When she failed eighth grade, for example, Loretta merely returned to school to repeat the grade, even though many of her friends were dropping out. Not long after that, however, she met a man named Oliver "Mooney" Lynn. The couple married in 1948, when Loretta was only thirteen years old. They moved to Custer, Washington, and began raising a family.

All the while, though, Loretta held on to her dream of becoming a professional singer. She had sung in church when she was younger, and it was obvious that she had talent. So, after several years of diapers and dishes (she and Mooney had four children), Loretta began to perform. She started out in local clubs, fronting a band that included her brother Jay Lee Webb. Mooney later entered Loretta in a talent contest hosted by Buck Owens, and her performance there led to a guest spot on Owens's local television show. The owner of Zero Records saw the show, and soon Loretta had a recording contract. Her first single, "I'm a Honky Tonk Girl," was released in 1960. In October of that year, after moving to Nashville, Loretta performed the song on the Grand Ole Opry. Two years later she was invited to join the Opry cast.

Loretta's first major-label release, "Success" on Decca Records, reached No. 6 on the country charts in 1962. Over the better part of the next two decades she released a string of hit records that carried her to the top of the country music world. She has recorded more than sixty hit records as a solo artist and nearly two dozen more with duet partners Ernest Tubb and Conway Twitty. Among her most popular tunes are "You Ain't Woman Enough," "The Pill," "Don't Come Home A Drinkin'," "One's on the Way," "Love Is the Foundation," "Blue Kentucky Girl" and, of course, "Coal Miner's Daughter." Her pairing with Twitty produced five consecutive No. 1 singles in the early 1970s: "After the Fire Is Gone," "Lead Me On," "Louisiana Woman, Mississippi Man," "As Soon as I Hang Up the Phone" and "Feelin's."

Loretta has won dozens of country music awards. A true trailblazer, in 1972 she became the first woman to be named Entertainer of the Year by the Country Music Association, and in 1975 she became the first woman to be similarly honored by the Academy of Country Music. Both the ACM and *Music City News* have honored Loretta with Lifetime Achievement Awards. She is also a member of the Country Music Hall of Fame.

Three of country's classiest ladies: Reba McEntire, Loretta Lynn and Patty Loveless

Loretta

Remembers . . .

A few years ago, a fellow offered me a song called "They Don't Make 'Em Like My Daddy." All I heard was the title, and I knew I just had to make that record, because that's how I feel about my daddy, who died when he a young man around fifty-one years old. Even though he died before I ever got started singing, in 1959, I feel like Daddy's been the most important person in my life.

We've got some pictures of Daddy, and he's usually got this straight face on him, not much emotion. Mountain people are like that. It's hard to read 'em if you don't know 'em. He was real shy, not like people from the coal camps who are used to talking with each other. But Butcher's Holler was his kind of world. There, he was the greatest man you ever saw. He could fix anything with those wiry arms of his. He could hammer up a well box, or a fence for the hog, or a new outhouse. You had to do things for yourself in the hollers or you'd die.

Daddy couldn't get much work during the Depression, and we didn't have money. I remember one Chrismas when Daddy had only thirty-six cents for four children. Somehow, he managed to buy a little something for each of us down at the general store. He gave me a little plastic doll about three inches high, and I loved it like it was my own baby.

—From *Coal Miner's Daughter*,
by Loretta Lynn and George Vecsey

BARBARA
Mandrell

*T*HE FIRST TWO-TIME winner of the Country Music Association's
Entertainer of the Year award, Barbara Mandrell is a diminutive woman
(just five feet tall) whose stature belies her enormous drive and talent.
She was born into a family of musicians (her mother played accordion; her father
owned a music store and played guitar) on Christmas Day in 1948, and was playing
accordion and reading music by the time she was five years old. Within a few years she
would add pedal steel guitar, banjo, saxophone and bass to her repertoire.

Success came early to Barbara. She made her television debut at age eleven on a local
program in Los Angeles called *Town Hall Party*, and a year later appeared on ABC's

Five Star Jubilee. She was a featured performer in a Las Vegas nightclub show and she toured with the likes of Johnny Cash and Tex Ritter. At fourteen she became part of The Mandrells, a family band that included her father, Irby, who played guitar and sang; her mother, Mary Ellen, on bass; and Barbara on pedal steel guitar and saxophone. Another band member, Ken Dudney, played drums. The band toured in the United States and in Asia for a few years, but in 1967 Barbara and Dudney married, and Barbara quit show business to concentrate on being a homemaker.

What was supposed to be a retirement, however, turned out to be little more than a respite. During a visit to the Grand Ole Opry, Barbara felt the urge to perform once again, and by 1969 she had signed a recording contract with Columbia Records and hit the charts for the first time with a cover of the Otis Redding song "I've Been Loving You Too Long." The following year she tasted success again with "Playin' Around With Love." On July 29, 1972, Barbara joined the cast of the Grand Ole Opry.

After she switched to ABC-Dot in 1975, Barbara's career really took off. "Standing Room Only" became her first Top 5 single, and in 1978 she reached No. 1 with "Sleeping Single in a Double Bed." That was the beginning of a sustained period of popularity, stretching into the mid-1980s, during which Barbara was one of the hottest performers in country or popular music. Among her No.1 singles were "If Loving You Is Wrong, I Don't Want to Be Right," "Years," "I Was Country When Country Wasn't Cool," "Till You're Gone" and "One of a Kind Pair of Fools."

Not satisfied with merely achieving massive success as a recording artist, Barbara branched out in the eighties. She was a frequent performer on television shows and served as cohost of the Academy of Country Music Awards. In 1980 NBC gave her a weekly network platform on which to display her skills, in a musical variety show titled *Barbara Mandrell and the Mandrell Sisters*, which also featured her younger siblings, Louise and Irlene.

But life hasn't been entirely kind to Barbara. Her strength and character were severely tested in 1982, when vocal strain forced a curtailment of her performing schedule, including the cancellation of her television show. Two years later Barbara and two of her children were involved in an automobile accident. All three suffered serious injuries that required long periods of rehabilitation. Barbara did eventually return to the stage, however, and in 1990 she published her autobiography, *Get to the Heart: My Story*.

In addition to her CMA Entertainer of the Year awards, Barbara has twice been named CMA Female Vocalist of the Year. She has also received the TNN–*Music City News* Living Legend Award.

Barbara

Remembers . . .

I have always thought it was the greatest honor to be born on my Savior's birthday. Even as a child, we separated those two days. First came Jesus. We would thank God for the gift of Jesus, and we would bake a birthday cake for Him and blow out the candles. Only later, at three o'clock in the afternoon, would we celebrate my birthday with another cake and more candles. And we still do that in my family. My children bake two cakes, one for Jesus and one for me. Without him, there would be no me.

Our childhood was a happy blur of homemade cookies and pretty dresses, church and company, little shows we would improvise in the living room, animals all over the place, bandages and bruises, games and music. I can tell you our childhood was not very different from what we did on television for two seasons. Holidays were played out like a ritual supplied by a scriptwriter. We all had our roles. Daddy has always been terrible about having to know what you have bought for him. He cannot wait. One Christmas, I bought him an engraved gold lighter, and I hid it in a shoebox, and wrapped it, and put it in a grocery bag, and put it in a bigger box, which drove him nuts.

Now, I should never have been this stupid, but one day I picked up the phone and a high-pitched voice said, "Hi, what'd you get your daddy for Christmas?" and I said, "A gold lighter," and the voice dropped a few octaves and said, "Thank you very much." Nowadays, whenever he wants to tease me, Daddy will say, "What'd you get your daddy for Christmas?"

—FROM *Get to the Heart: My Story*,
BY BARBARA MANDRELL WITH GEORGE VECSEY

The Grand Ole Opry Country Christmas Album

Barbara Mandrell

KATHY
Mattea

"**I'VE ALWAYS SAID** that life is like a blank canvas. And at the end, you don't want to have nothing on it."

Kathy Mattea has spent the better part of the last two decades filling her canvas with stark and dramatic images. A fearless artist, her ever-shifting musical tastes over the years have resulted in an impressive and eclectic catalog of recordings. Traditional country, bluegrass, folk, Celtic—all can be found in the discography of Kathy Mattea. "I believe music is music," Kathy said after the release of her 1997 album, the soulful and overtly spiritual *Love Travels*. "This album is part of my musical progression. It's all about a musical journey."

That journey began in earnest when Kathy began playing guitar and taking voice lessons in junior high. Later, as an engineering student at the University of West Virginia, she joined a bluegrass band called Pennsboro. After two years of school, with music having taken hold of her heart, Kathy dropped out and moved to Nashville. Like most newcomers to Music City, Kathy struggled to make a living. She supported herself as a waitress and tour guide at the Country Music Hall of Fame before graduating to steady work singing jingles and demos.

Kathy's first big break came in 1982, when she joined Bobby Goldsboro's touring company, and within two years she had a contract with Mercury Records. In 1984, two singles from her eponymous debut album, "Street Talk" and "Someone Is Falling in Love," hit the U.S. country charts and helped establish Kathy as a formidable new artist. Her second album, 1985's *From My Heart*, yielded three more hit singles, and 1986's *Walk the Way the Wind Blows*, which featured a cover version of Nanci Griffith's "Love at the Five and Dime," boosted her reputation even further. But it was the 1987 release of *Untasted Honey* that made Kathy a household name among country music fans. The album contained the No. 1 hits "Goin' Gone" and "Eighteen Wheels and a Dozen Roses," the latter of which earned Single of the Year and Song of the Year honors from the Academy of Country Music.

Willow in the Wind, released in 1989, was equally successful. It featured the crossover hit "Where've You Been?", which was named Song of the Year by both the ACM and the Country Music Association. Kathy was named Female Vocalist of the Year by the CMA in 1989 and 1990, and won Grammy Awards in 1990 (Best Country Performance) and 1993 (Best Southern Gospel, Country Gospel or Bluegrass Gospel Album).

Kathy
Remembers . . .

Whent people ask me about my favorite Christmas memory, I always go back to this one particular year, because it really does stand out. When I was young, my family always had a family reunion on Christmas Eve. And it was at our house. It was this great night when the house filled up with people and food and presents and kids. You eat and you open presents and it's really fun. Then you go to sleep and when you wake up the next morning, Santa has come. This was my favorite twenty-four hours on the face of the earth. And this had gone on my whole life. I have two older brothers, and none of us had ever missed this party. But when I moved to Nashville, after I'd been here a couple years, I got a job as a waitress, and it was at a restaurant where you could make good money. And I really needed the job at the time. Well, because I had started in October, by December 1 was still one of the "new guys," and I could not get Christmas Eve off. So I called home and said, "I've tried everything, but there's no one to work for me. I can make it home on Christmas Day, but I can't get home on Christmas Eve."

This was the first time anyone in our family was going to have to miss the party. I had just turned twenty-one, and I hadn't been that far away from home for very long, and it was a very tough thing for me to accept. But then, at the last minute, like two days before, a guy came up to me and said, "Look, I'll work Christmas Eve for you. It's fine. Go home and see your family." He was so sweet. So I decided not to tell them I was coming. I picked up the phone and called my sister-in-law so that someone would know I was going to be on the road that night, because it was supposed to snow, but I didn't tell anyone else. I drove all day, eight hours, from Nashville to West Virginia.

And I had this funky old car, one of those cars that had been passed around to everybody's kids. But it made the trip fine. I pulled up just about the time the party was kicking into high gear, and I parked at the bottom of the hill, so that no one would see me, and I walked up to the house. I walked around to the back door and stepped into the kitchen and said, "Hey, you know where you can get a drink around here?"

My mother looked like she had seen a ghost. She couldn't believe it. The entire family was there, and it was like . . . instant hugs from fifteen people. My mother just kept looking at me. She'd hug me and look at me, hug me and look at me. She couldn't believe I was there. It was great. Then I went down in the basement to see my dad, who had broken his leg and wasn't supposed to walk at all. But when he saw me, he got up to run across the room, and they had to hold him back to keep him from running on his broken leg.

It was wonderful. It was everything that you think of Christmas being about. I was on the cusp of adulthood, going back to this tradition from my childhood. I was off on my own and I'd made this break and moved to Nashville to try my hand at music, but I was still kind of scared, and this was like going back to the womb, to the security of my family. All of that was rolled into one great moment.

Kathy's
Favorite Christmas Song

I have a favorite Christmas song, and it's called "Mary, Did You Know?" I made a Christmas album in 1992, and it actually won a Grammy in the gospel category. And this song was on it. It was a song a friend of mine turned me onto, and it was written by Buddy Green and Mark Lowry. It's about the moment just after Jesus is born; an angel comes down and whispers into Mary's ear and says, "This is your little baby, but did you know that he's going to walk on water? Did you know that he will heal people? Blind people will see, and deaf people will hear because of him." It's a powerful song.

REBA

McEntire

ALTHOUGH THE ODDS against a kid who grew up on an Oklahoma ranch making it to the top of the music world would seem to be pretty steep, Reba Nell McEntire never wavered in her quest. Perhaps that's because taking risks has always come naturally to her. The daughter of Clark McEntire, a professional rodeo competitor, Reba learned at a young age how to ride a horse and rope a steer. In the process she learned how to tame her fears and become comfortable with the idea of competing and performing. From her mother, Jackie, she inherited a love for music and an appreciation of the hard work required to become a polished singer.

Reba participated in rodeo events while she was growing up, but she also sang with her sisters, Susie and Alice, and her brother, Pake. They eventually formed a group and recorded a song titled "The Ballad of John McEntire," about their grandfather. The tune received airplay on a local level and inspired the McEntire children to pursue loftier goals. They planned to form a professional group, but those plans were sidetracked in 1974 when Reba was asked to sing the National Anthem at the National Rodeo Finals in Oklahoma City. Her rendition of "The Star-Spangled Banner" was so impressive that one member of the audience, honky-tonk singer Red Steagall, suggested she move to Nashville. With Steagall's assistance, Reba landed her first recording contract just one year later, with Mercury Records.

Although her first single, "I Don't Want to Be a One-Night Stand," made the country charts in 1976, it took several years for Reba to find the vast, mainstream audience that she enjoys today. Thanks in part to a decision to concentrate on ballads that showcased her powerful voice, Reba's career began to pick up steam at the end of the decade. In 1982 she had her first No. 1 single, "Can't Even Get the Blues." She followed that up with "You're the First Time I've Thought About Leaving," which reached the top of the country charts in 1983. The following year Reba moved to MCA Records and embarked on one of the longest hot streaks in the history of country music. Among the hits that catapulted her to superstardom were "Just a Little Love," "Have I Got a New Deal for You" and "Whoever's in New England." By 1990 Reba had sold more than twenty million records. Between 1985 and 1992 she hit the Top 10 with twenty-four consecutive single releases; she reached No. 1 on fourteen separate occasions.

Although Reba branched out in the 1990s, allowing pop and rock to more heavily influence her work with releases such as "For My Broken Heart" and "The Fear of Being Alone," she remains one of country music's most popular and successful artists. She has also penned a bestselling autobiography and become a successful actress in both feature films (the cult horror classic *Tremors*, *The Little Rascals* and Rob Reiner's *North*) and made-for-television movies (*The Man from Left Field*, with Burt Reynolds; *Buffalo Girls*, with Anjelica Huston and Melanie Griffith; and *Is There Life Out There*, based on her own hit song).

One of the most acclaimed performers in country music, Reba has won two Grammy Awards, six Country Music Association awards and 10 Academy of Country Music awards. She has been a member of the Grand Ole Opry since January 14, 1986.

Reba

Remembers . . .

Christmas is my favorite holiday, mainly because I get a chance to spend a lot of time with family and friends, and because it's also my time off. Christmas has been even more enjoyable since I had Shelby, my son. He's now nine years old, and he's so wonderful to be around. Little kids are just so much fun—they're the most incredible things in the world. Sometimes I don't know what I did before Shelby came along.

Anyway, one year we were in Aspen at Christmastime. Having grown up in Oklahoma and Texas, [my husband] Narvel and I never had white Christmases, so we loved to go to Colorado. Well, one Christmas Eve it was just Narvel and Shelby and I in Aspen. We had gone out on Christmas Eve to eat dinner. And we hadn't gotten Shelby anything for Christmas yet, because with all our relatives and friends buying for him . . . well, he gets quite a bit. He gets plenty of stuff. This was when he was only about three or four years old. So we got something to eat and then walked across the street to this little toy shop. We walked around in the toy store for a while, and I looked around and shouted, "Hey, Shelby, let's go back to where the Nintendo games are!" And he walked over and said, "Oh, Mom, look." And there was this little metal tractor-trailer. It was the nicest one I'd ever seen. It was very well-built.

Shelby just stared at it. Then he looked up at me and said, "Oh, Mom, I just wuv this." That's the way he was talking then: "wuv."

So we walked around the store a little bit more, but I couldn't get him away from the tractor-trailer. Finally, Narvel whispered, "Get him out of the store so I can buy it." So I walked with Shelby down to the next store, but he kept going on and on about this tractor-trailer.

"Well, maybe Santa Claus will get it for you," I said. "But right now, let's go down and get you a pair of snow boots, because that's what you really need."

He shook his head. "No, Mom, I just wuv that tractor. Can we go back and get it?"

"Maybe tomorrow," I said. "Or maybe Santa Claus will get it for you."

As we were driving back to the house, something must have dawned on Shelby, because he said, "Mom, how will Santa Claus know?" And I said, "Shelby . . . Santa Claus does carry a cellular phone, you know."

"Does he really?"

"Oh, yeah. I'll bet you anything that store manager saw you looking at that tractor-trailer and now he's gonna call Santa Claus."

So we went home and sang Christmas songs and had a great time. Narvel and I put out the cookies and the milk, and Shelby helped us get everything ready, and we wrote the note to Santa Claus, and Shelby went to bed. The next morning that little face was right in my face, right beside my bed. I opened my eyes and there he was, big-eyed, and he said, "Mom, you're not gonna believe what happened!"

"What?"

"Santa Claus brought my tractor-trailer!"

I said, "Are you serious?" And Shelby said, "Uh-huh. Come here. Get up, Daddy, let's go look!"

So we got up and walked out into the living room, and right there, sitting on the hearth of the fireplace, was that tractor-trailer. And all the cookies and milk were gone.

To this day, Shelby is a believer in Santa Claus. In fact, we all are.

The Grand Ole Opry Country Christmas Album

Reba McEntire

LORRIE
Morgan

ONE OF THE top-selling female artists in country music history, Lorrie Morgan was seemingly born to be a star. Her full name, after all, is Loretta Lynn Morgan. And her father, George Morgan, was a legendary country singer and a member of the Grand Ole Opry for twenty-six years, until his death in 1975. Lorrie naturally spent a lot of time around the music business; she also spent a lot of time backstage at the Opry, watching her dad work. Lorrie was only thirteen years old when she made her Opry debut. With her father at the edge of the stage, crying out of sheer joy and pride, Lorrie overcame a serious case of the jitters and sang her heart out. She was so impressive that the crowd gave her a standing ovation.

Lorrie's career was launched that night, of course, but it wasn't until four years later that she began singing professionally. By the time she was twenty-one, Lorrie was opening for the likes of George Jones. By twenty-four she was a star in her own right, as evidenced by her induction into the Grand Ole Opry on June 9, 1984. Lorrie has had a string of hits over the years, including "Train Wreck of Emotion," and "Till a Tear Becomes a Rose," a duet with her husband, Keith Whitley, whose brilliant career ended tragically with his death in 1989. That same year, Lorrie released the single "Dear Me," which catapulted her to superstardom. A versatile and daring musician with eclectic tastes, Lorrie has collaborated with a wide range of vocalists over the years, including Andy Williams, Tammy Wynette, Frank Sinatra, Johnny Mathis, Sammy Kershaw and the Beach Boys.

A self-professed lover of "big ballads and glamour," Lorrie is a four-time winner of the TNN–*Music City News* Female Vocalist Award.

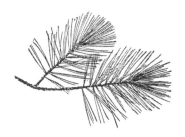

Lorrie

Remembers . . .

My dad was on the road almost 300 days a year when I was growing up, but he always made it a point to be home for holidays, especially Christmas. So Christmas, to me, didn't just mean Santa Claus was coming—it meant Dad was coming! And Dad was going to be there for a while. So it was a double treat. The icing on the cake at Christmas was that Dad was there.

Being a Catholic family, we always planned Christmas Eve around midnight mass. But Dad would never go to midnight mass with us. Well, he went once in a while, but most of the time he stayed home, because he got scared leaving the house at night with all the gifts in there. He was worried about someone breaking in and taking all the presents. A couple times we even had someone else come over and watch the house so that Dad could go to midnight mass with us. One thing that was great was that we always got to open a little gift on Christmas Eve, before going off to mass, and it was always something nice that we could wear to church. That was exciting. I remember when I was little we'd come out of midnight mass every year and it would be snowing. We had so many white Christmases when I was a little girl, but now, with the change in the ozone or whatever, we very seldom see a white Christmas in Nashville anymore, which is a shame. But it was always the most wonderful time of the year for a wide-eyed child, to walk out of midnight mass, and it's snowing, and your dad is home, and your mom is home, and tomorrow you're opening your gifts and you're having a big Christmas dinner! It was beautiful.

Dad was such a great creator of make-believe for us kids. He delighted in watching children get excited and believing in the magic of Christmas and Santa. He and Mom would put little surprises around the house. Like, if we were good before Christmas, we'd

Lorrie Morgan

get up and there would be a surprise from the elves in our stockings, and a note saying, "You were good last night so here's a gift for you." My dad just delighted in watching that sort of thing, and creating it. We would all be sitting in the living room around the tree, and all of a sudden candy would start flying through the room. Of course, being little, we didn't know Dad was standing behind something throwing it at us. We thought the elves were showering us with candy. It was just the most magical time of our lives when Dad was home creating Christmas for us. And he always showered my mom with wonderful gifts. She always had the most presents on Christmas morning. It would take her about an hour to open her presents because Dad would bring her stuff from every nook and cranny in the United States and Europe.

Lorrie's
Favorite Christmas Song

I grew up thinking Santa Claus was the greatest thing in the world, and my dad was a big reason for that. He wrote the song "Up on Santa Claus Mountain" for us children when we were little. And he'd sing it every year. He'd sit there with his guitar at Christmastime and sing for hours for the family. That song had never been recorded; he just wrote it for us children. Many years later, when I went in to record my own Christmas album, *Merry Christmas from London*, we had nothing with his song on it, which was sad. But my uncle Francis, who has since passed away, had an old copy of a tape at his house, of Dad sitting in his living room, with his guitar, singing "Up on Santa Claus Mountain." And that's how we were able to record the song for my album. All of us children just remembered it in bits and pieces, and we were trying to fit it together—this goes here, this goes there—but thanks to my uncle we were able to put it all together. We gave the tape to the symphony in London and they created this beautiful version of "Up on Santa Claus Mountain" for my album. The cool thing is, the recitation in the version of the song that appears on my album involving the St. Joseph's Children's Choir, I wrote that. Dad wrote the melody and the other lyrics, and I wrote the recitation, so it really was a collaboration between the two of us.

JIMMY C.
Newman

JIMMY YVES NEWMAN grew up in the heart of Cajun country, which only partially explains why his popular band is named Cajun Country. The real answer stems from the fact that no one is quite as adept as Jimmy at combining traditional country music with the sound of the Louisiana bayou. The Alligator Man is truly an original.

Jimmy first developed an interest in music while listening to his older brother Walter play guitar. Jimmy joined a local Cajun band when he was a teenager and soon began playing in clubs throughout the state. Eventually he was given an opportunity to host his own radio show in Lake Charles, Louisiana, and in the early 1950s he signed a recording contract with Dot Records. Four years later Jimmy had his first hit single, "Cry, Cry Darling," which reached No. 4 on the country charts and helped him land a spot on the popular radio and television show *Louisiana Hayride.* He placed five records in the Top 10 between 1955 and 1957, including "A Fallen Star," which reached No. 1 on the country charts and became a hit with pop audiences as well.

Jimmy added a "C" to his name when one of his drummers began calling him Jimmy "Cajun" Newman. It was appropriate not only because of Jimmy's background, but because he continued to wear his Cajun influence proudly as a musician. He had hits with the Cajun-flavored "Alligator Man" in 1961 and "Bayou Talk" in 1962. In 1963 he released the album *Folk Songs of the Bayou.* Jimmy formed Cajun Country in 1978, and the band quickly established a loyal following while performing such traditional favorites as "Jole Blon," "Jambalaya" and "The Cajun Stripper." Cajun Country was nominated for a Grammy Award in 1991, the same year in which Jimmy teamed up with Doug Kershaw, Eddy Raven and others for the first Cajun Fest.

Jimmy C. Newman was inducted into the Grand Ole Opry in August 1956.

Jimmy C.

Remembers . . .

We were brought up very, very poor. Christmas was Christmas, and it was oranges and it was apples and popcorn decorations, and a green pine tree for a Christmas tree. It was the decorations that represented Christmas more than anything else. I remember one Christmas I got a cap pistol, and another time my big deal was a little green automobile, about eight to ten inches long with a flashlight battery underneath the hood and two flashlight bulbs for headlights. That was a very big thing for a little kid.

My dad, you see, was an invalid. At seven months he had polio, so life was hard for him. But he raised three different families in spite of that. At the time I was growing up he was on crutches. But we ran a country store, so he would travel by mules and wagon fifteen miles each way to trade groceries. Like, for instance, he'd take in chickens and eggs in payment for groceries, and then he'd go trade them at the big store in town. He did that most every day, except on weekends. Mom took care of me as best she could, and she ran the store, and she also had a garden. In the deep South you had a lot of that—someone surviving off a garden and some chickens, and of course we had a store, so we were lucky, really.

I do remember when I was about five or six years old there was a two-room schoolhouse, and one of the rooms was used as an auditorium. There was a stage . . . and a Christmas tree up there on the stage. Very pretty. And I remember the trees we had in our house—the smell, the way they looked. We always had pine, because there were a lot of pine trees where I grew up. And they were always decorated with a lot of popcorn.

Jimmy C. Newman

Getting the tree was a real chore, of course, because my father couldn't cut down the tree. So my brother usually did it. When I got old enough, I helped out.

As for when my son was growing up, a lot of time we'd go back to Louisiana for Christmas, for a real Cajun Christmas. It can get pretty exciting, let me tell you, but for us it was just nice to get back to be with kin. The food was always great; there's nothing like Cajun food. And I don't want to say there was a lot of celebrating . . . but Cajuns do celebrate. It was always a lot of fun.

Jimmy's
Favorite Christmas Song

My niece and I wrote one not long ago, which is my favorite now, called "Joyeaux Noel." You see it on Christmas cards a lot. And it was recorded by Louise Mandrell on one of her more recent albums. My niece writes for a company here in town, and the guy who runs the company is an old friend of mine. He asked us if we could come up with a Cajun Christmas song, and that's what we did.

THE
Osborne Brothers

Bobby Osborne
Sonny Osborne

INSTRUMENTAL VIRTUOSOS AND vocal innovators, the Osborne Brothers were weaned on the folk ballads and coal-mining songs of their native Kentucky. Although they would come to be regarded as one of the great bluegrass duos, the brothers actually followed separate paths early in their careers. This was primarily a function of the difference in their ages.

Sonny was eleven years old when he persuaded his father to buy him his first banjo, a $100 Kay five-string. By the time the banjo arrived in the mail, Sonny had already figured out how to play two songs, "We'll Be Sweethearts in Heaven" and "Cripple Creek." He fell in love with everything about the instrument and often practiced well into the predawn hours. Sonny later began playing with some local musicians and, as a teenager, sharpened his skills at the knee of none other than Bill Monroe, the father of bluegrass music. Sonny was only fourteen years old when he joined Monroe and the Bluegrass Boys for an appearance on the Grand Ole Opry.

While Sonny was first learning how to play banjo, older brother Bobby was making a name for himself playing guitar and mandolin in West Virginia as a member of the Lonesome Pine Fiddlers. He later started a band called the Sunny Mountain Boys that played at radio station WCYB, along with such bluegrass luminaries as Jim & Jesse, and Lester Flatt and Earl Scruggs.

It wasn't until 1953, after Bobby served in the Korean War, that the Osborne Brothers finally hooked up. Their first major-label release, on MGM Records, came in 1956. With their unique harmonies and mesmerizing instrumental skill, the Osborne Brothers became one of the most popular bluegrass bands of the time, and one of the most influential groups the genre has ever known. In the 1960s they left MGM for Decca Records and began experimenting with a bigger, fuller sound that included a steel guitar, piano and electric instruments, which helped them gain access to a mainstream country audience. Among their many hit records were "Up This Hill and Down," "Midnight Flyer," "Making Plans," "Ruby," "Muddy Bottom" and, of course, "Rocky Top," which became Tennessee's official state song and the unofficial anthem for University of Tennessee athletic teams.

The Osborne Brothers have been members of the Grand Ole Opry since August 8, 1964.

Sonny
Remembers . . .

Bobby and I had the typical Christmas when we were kids. In our early lives, things were pretty rough, and we didn't get very much. That's just the way it was. But the main thing I remember about Christmas, the one that sticks in my mind the most, came after we had been in this business for a while. You see, on Christmas Day, 1967, "Rocky Top" was released. And, of course, "Rocky Top" was our signature song and the biggest thing that ever happened for us. The song has been recorded more than a thousand times, and it's sold countless millions of records, and we were there at the beginning.

The funny thing is, it really wasn't that big a deal at the time, except that in all of our business career—and we've been dealing with record companies in one form or another since 1953—I haven't talked to anyone else who remembers a song being released on Christmas Day. I'm sure there have been others, but I don't know of them, and I've never talked to anyone who knows of another. But the release date on "Rocky Top" was 12/25/67. Why they did that, I have no idea.

I didn't hear it on the radio until a week or so after Christmas, and by then we knew we had something special. The writer, Boudleaux Bryant, called and told me the song was a tremendous hit. See, Bobby and I had a record contract coming up that we had to sign the first of the year, so Decca didn't tell us anything about it, that it was going to be a hit song. Boudleaux and Felice Bryant called me the next week and said that it had sold, I think, something like 85,000 records in less than 10 days. Bobby and I were shocked, because we really didn't have any expectations for the record. We thought it was a good bluegrass song, and that's about it. We were actually pushing the other side, a song called "My Favorite Memory." It was a fluke thing that we recorded "Rocky Top," anyway. I went over to Boudleaux's house on a Sunday—he lived close to me and was a very good friend of mine—and he said he had this song he wanted me to hear. So he played "Rocky Top," and I listened to it and thought, Well, I guess it's a good, typical bluegrass song—nothing more. I called Bobby and he came over and listened to it, too. We both sort of liked it, but we didn't jump up and down or anything. I said to Boudleaux, "I'll tell you what—we're gonna rehearse about 9:30 Wednesday morning. If you bring a copy of this song, and we can get it down, then we'll go ahead and cut it that afternoon." And that's what we did.

That's what makes this business what it is. It's intriguing, because nobody can pinpoint anything. "Rocky Top" was the greatest Christmas present we've ever received. What more could anybody want? Anyone who ever picks up an instrument, who ever plays at the Grand Ole Opry or ever is any kind of musician, should have that happen once in his life, just to get that feeling. It's incredible.

The Grand Ole Opry Country Christmas Album

Sonny's
Favorite Christmas Song

I guess my favorite Christmas song is "Silver Bells." I don't even know why. I just like it a lot. And Anne Murray's recording of it is my favorite.

BASHFUL BROTHER
Oswald

WHEN BASHFUL BROTHER Oswald was inducted into the Grand Ole Opry on January 21, 1995, he said, "I'm the happiest man alive." Then, with a laugh, he added, "You know, I've been auditioning for this part for fifty-six years."

Just about. "Os" was eighty-three years old at the time, a man with a long and rich musical legacy who had entertained generations of country music fans. The son of an Appalachian musician, he was born Beecher Ray Kirby. Friends called him "Pete" when he was growing up, and he developed a love for music at an early age. By the time he was in his teens and working at a local sawmill, Pete was earning extra cash playing banjo, guitar and Dobro, or singing gospel music at local clubs.

Kirby later took a job at an auto plant in Flint, Michigan. He lost his job during the Depression, and wound up supporting himself as a musician at radio station WFDF. In 1934 he moved to Knoxville, Tennessee, and quickly found work playing Dobro with various bands, including one fronted by the legendary Roy Acuff. He joined Acuff's Smoky Mountain Boys on January 8, 1939, and over the years became one of the act's most popular and enduring performers. Kirby was a multitalented artist who not only played guitar, banjo, jug and Dobro, but also sang tenor and skillfully executed comedy skits. The band's lead singer, Rachel Veach, often referred to Kirby as her "great big Bashful Brother Oswald," and the nickname—and character—stuck. Bashful Brother Oswald appeared onstage in a floppy hat, baggy overalls and enormous shoes. His laugh was a deep-throated howl.

If audiences loved the cartoonish character of Bashful Brother Oswald, they also appreciated his exquisite musicianship. Even as a supporting artist, his talent was evident, and his influence on younger musicians would be felt for decades. In 1972, for example, he played on *Will the Circle Be Unbroken*, the hit album by the Nitty Gritty Dirt Band. As Acuff once said of his bandmate, "I don't think anyone has the style, the touch and the control of a Dobro instrument like Oswald. I don't think anyone has even come close to him in his type of playing. Os is the best."

Oswald played with Acuff through the mid-1980s. By the 1960s, though, he was also putting together an impressive career as a solo artist. He worked as a session musician and released several albums, including *Bashful Brother Oswald*, *That's Country*, *Banjo and Dobro* and *Don't Say Aloha*.

Bashful Brother Oswald's popularity extends well beyond the country music world. When he was inducted into the Grand Ole Opry, he received letters of congratulations from, among others, President Bill Clinton, Vice President Al Gore, Tennessee governor Don Sundquist, and fellow artists Dolly Parton, Travis Tritt and Willie Nelson. In Nashville, Mayor Phil Bredesen declared January 21 to be Bashful Brother Oswald Day. Os published his autobiography, *That's the Truth if I've Ever Told It*, in 1994. In January 1999 he celebrated sixty years of entertaining fans at the Grand Ole Opry.

Bashful Brother Oswald

Remembers . . .

What do I remember from my Christmas in the Smokies? Well, I was the fifth of ten children, so Christmas was kind of slim at our house, at least as far as gifts were concerned. We always got fruit and a new pair of shoes, and the older boys would get a new pair of boots for the winter. But we always had our music, and that was important. My dad and all eight of us boys played, and my two sisters would sing. It was wonderful.

Before each Christmas we'd go into the woods and cut down our own special Christmas tree. Then we'd decorate it with strings of popcorn. We would save our chewing gum wrappers throughout the year, and gather the sycamore balls and wrap them up and hang them on the tree. For added effect, we'd drape cotton over the tree to look like snow.

Christmas was a happy time of year in our house. When I think of the holiday, I think of going to church, playing our music and the family being together. About the only time I've been away at Christmastime was during World War II, when I was playing with Roy Acuff. We spent most of our holidays entertaining servicemen. Even though I was away from my family, I enjoyed that, because I knew how important it was.

BRAD
Paisley

THROUGH A COMBINATION of diligence and good fortune, Brad Paisley has become one of the hottest young stars in country music. The West Virginia native received his first guitar, a Sears Danelectro Silvertone with an amp in the case, when he was just eight years old. The presenter of that gift was Brad's grandfather, a railman who worked the night shift and spent his afternoons playing guitar. Brad often sat at his grandfather's knee, listening to the old man trying to mimic the genius of Les Paul, Chet Atkins and Merle Travis.

Brad began performing in front of audiences when he was ten. He started out singing and playing guitar at his church. Pretty soon he was performing at birthday parties and holiday events all over the region. Brad wrote his first song, "Born on Christmas Day," when he was twelve. By thirteen he was a regular performer on Wheeling's *Jamboree USA*, and in his spare time he opened for such renowned artists as George Jones, The Judds, Steve Wariner and Ricky Skaggs.

While attending Belmont University in Nashville, Brad served an internship at ASCAP. A friend there introduced him to talent scouts at EMI Music, and within a week after graduation, Brad had a songwriting contract with the company. He later signed a recording contract with Arista Records, which released his acclaimed debut album, *Who Needs Pictures*, in 1999. The album climbed into the Top 10, and spawned his first No. 1 song—"He Didn't Have to Be"—and solidified Brad's reputation as an artist who bears close watching in the new millennium. He has performed at the Grand Ole Opry more than twenty-five times in his young career.

Brad

Remembers . . .

When I was home on Christmas break during my sophomore year in college, I was working part-time at a resort near Wheeling, West Virginia. I was singing Christmas songs throughout the week as a way to make some extra money during the holidays. I'd just sit there with a guitar and sing music for busloads of tourists coming through to see our festival of lights.

The place where I would sing had a roaring fireplace. It was a really nice, cozy atmosphere. But I usually had some other sort of engagement later that same evening, whether it be at a bar or a country dance hall or whatever. And walking out into the cold every night, I ended up with an ear infection. My doctor put me on antibiotics for the ear infection, and it did the job pretty well. In just a couple days I was doing a lot better and thought everything was getting back to normal. In fact, on December 23rd, the night before Christmas Eve, I went to bed feeling fine. But when I woke up on the 24th, I could hardly get out of bed. After a while I dragged myself downstairs and sat on the couch, but I couldn't go any farther. I was just completely exhausted. I was totally winded and sick and couldn't understand why I felt so bad.

My parents could tell right away something was wrong, and they insisted I go see a doctor. So I did. It turned out that I had pneumonia and had to be admitted to Wheeling Hospital that very day. What had happened, apparently, was that the antibiotic I'd been given had completely wiped out the ear problem—but the infection had come back as pneumonia. At that time of year in my home area, with all the power plants and coal mines and everything, the air is not always the best; it's a real industrial area. A lot of times when you get a cold you wind up getting a cough, too. And in my case it had led to pneumonia.

So I spent December 24th until December 27th in the hospital. I don't remember a whole lot about Christmas Day. I was out of it. I started to feel better on the 26th, after they put me on intravenous antibiotics. Pneumonia is a dangerous thing, and they weren't fooling around with it. A young girl right around my age had died of pneumonia just a couple weeks earlier, so the doctors in the area were being very cautious. Anybody who caught it was hospitalized immediately, and rightly so, because it's not anything to take lightly.

Anyway, while I was in the hospital I felt pretty sorry for myself. Here it was Christmas Day, and I was spending it in the hospital all by myself. Well, not really by myself—my parents and family would come by to see me, of course, but still . . . I was sick and in the hospital on Christmas. But as I started to feel better, they'd let me get out of bed and take short walks to keep the pneumonia from settling in my lungs. So I'd take long, slow walks down the hall. And while taking these walks I would meet some folks who were out taking their walks, too: elderly folks or even some young people like myself. A lot of the cancer patients were also on my floor, and I got to meet a lot of them. We talked a lot, and I got to find out that several of the folks on my floor were told that this would probably be their last Christmas. Now, here I am feeling sorry for myself because I had to stay in the hospital and miss Christmas at home, and here are these folks . . . and it's their last Christmas, and they're stuck in the hospital. A lot of those folks will never see another Christmas, and here they are getting needles shoved in their arms, they're taking all these medications and going through horrible procedures, and that's Christmas for them.

Everyone in my family waited until I got home on the 27th to open their presents. We celebrated Christmas all together. It still wasn't quite the same, of course; there's nothing quite like that feeling when you know it's Christmas Day. But at least my family was very good about making it good for me. And the point is: At least I got to go home.

I really feel like everything in our lives happens for a reason. Had I not spent that Christmas in the hospital like I did, Christmas would not mean half of what it does to me now. Every year when I wake up healthy on December 24th, and I'm able to go to church, and spend the time with my family doing things I want to do, I'm twice as thankful as I ever would have been. So I'm grateful I was given that illness; it taught me a lesson about what to be thankful for at Christmastime, and also our responsibility to people who are less fortunate than us at that time of year.

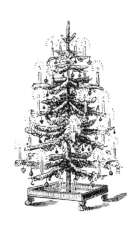

Brad Paisley

Brad's
Favorite Christmas Music

I just love "There's a New Kid in Town," by Keith Whitley. I always thought that was one of the coolest songs, and I always loved Keith Whitley. I've sung that song in church the last couple years when I've gone home. I just think it's great because it's a unique approach to a Christmas song. I think it's destined someday to be a classic holiday song. Every Christmas you start to hear songs more and more that are brand-new. I also really like Vince Gill's tribute to his brother, "Won't Be the Same This Year."

Also, I played a long-running show called *Jamboree USA*, and the reason I got on there is because the first song I ever wrote was a Christmas song called "Born on Christmas Day." It's actually not a bad song. I look back on it and I've written worse songs here in the last two weeks. And that one I wrote when I was twelve years old. I have a lot of tapes of that song, and we're trying to figure out a way that I can record that and save part of the original with me singing it. Maybe do a duet with myself. I sounded a lot more like Alison Krauss than George Strait back then.

DOLLY
Parton

DOLLY PARTON WAS born in a place unlikely to have produced one of America's best-known and most popular entertainers—a dirt-poor mountain community in Sevier County, Tennessee. Dolly was the fourth of twelve children born to a man who could neither read nor write. Her uncle gave her a guitar when she was just eight, and within a couple of years she was performing regularly on television and radio. Dolly made her debut on the Grand Ole Opry three years later; she moved to Nashville shortly after graduating from high school in 1964.

Dolly arrived in Music City with little more than a cardboard suitcase and a big dream, but she was lacking in neither talent nor ambition. She began peddling her songs to Nashville producers and record industry executives. Sometimes she'd show up with a demo; other times she'd charm her way through the front door and perform an impromptu concert, accompanying herself on guitar. For two years Dolly struggled to gain a measure of recognition, but had little success. In 1966, however, a song she penned for Bill Phillips, "Put It Off Until Tomorrow," landed in the Top 10, and soon Dolly was offered a recording contract with Monument Records. She recorded her first two hits, "Dumb Blonde" and "Something Fishy," in 1967.

That same year Porter Wagoner hired Dolly to replace Norma Jean as his sidekick and resident "girl singer" on his popular television show and in his touring company. The two subsequently teamed up on a series of hit singles, starting with "The Last Thing on My Mind." Their collaboration lasted six years before Dolly struck out on her own and found enormous success as a crossover artist who was adept at performing both country and pop tunes. Among her biggest hits were "Here You Come Again" and "9 to 5," the title song from the hit 1980 movie. Dolly starred in that film, along with Jane Fonda and Lily Tomlin, and also earned an Academy Award nomination for Best Song.

Although her trademark blonde hair and striking looks often draw the most attention, and occasionally overshadow the artist behind the entertainer, Dolly is, first and foremost, a songwriter. Her songs have long captivated both listeners and other artists with their sensitivity and keen insight into everyday life. As fellow Opry member Emmylou Harris once said about Dolly's song "To Daddy," "To me it's like an O. Henry short story. Dolly sets you up and then . . . whammo! She turns it all around. When I first heard it my lips were trembling and I was afraid I was gonna make a scene."

An astute businesswoman as well as an accomplished artist, Dolly added her name to Dollywood, an amusement park in Pigeon Forge, Tennessee. She has won just about every major award in country music, including six Grammy Awards and seven Country Music Association awards. In 1986 she was named Woman of the Year by *Ms.* magazine. Dolly has also written two books—her autobiography, *Dolly: My Life and Other Unfinished Business,* and a children's book, *A Coat of Many Colors.* She was inducted into the Grand Ole Opry on January 4, 1969, and joined the Country Music Hall of Fame in 1999.

Dolly
Remembers . . .

Christmas was a warm, wonderful time for us. Snow has a way of making even a humble shack look magical and inviting. Christmas will always be certain images to me: the glow of the fire through the windows, the crackle of a pine knot burning, even the smoke that seemed to reach out and pull you by the nose into the house. My most memorable Christmas was the one for which I personally received the least. When Mama and Daddy married, he was only seventeen and she was fifteen and they were both poor. Daddy had never been able to give Mama a wedding ring. One Christmas he gathered us all together and explained to those of us that were old enough to understand that there wouldn't be the usual store-bought gifts we had come to expect; this year all of the money had gone to buy Mama a ring. There was instead one gift for the person who could find the ring where Daddy had hidden it. This set off a frenzy of searching. Everyplace that could accommodate a ring was looked into. Of course, all of this was accompanied by wild guesses as to what the one gift might be and confident proclamations of what each searcher would do with the gift once he or she had won it.

Finally, someone found the ring and rushed it to Mama. Everybody shared Daddy's pride as he slipped it on her finger and a chorus of very genuine "oohs" and "aahs" went up. The "one gift," as it turned out, was a big box of chocolates that we could all share. That is Daddy's way. Those chocolates were so sweet they could make your teeth hurt, and so are the memories of that Christmas.

—FROM *Dolly: My Life and Other Unfinished Business*,
BY DOLLY PARTON

JOHNNY
PayCheck

A DIMINUTIVE MAN WHOSE stature belies his enormous talent and
ambition, Johnny PayCheck was born Donald Eugene Lytle in
Greenfield, Ohio. He was six years old when he picked up a guitar for
the first time; by the age of fifteen he was playing professionally and dreaming of following in the footsteps of his idol, Hank Williams.

Johnny's first big break came in the late 1950s, after he was discharged from the U.S.
Navy. He took a job playing bass and steel guitar and singing backup for the great
George Jones. At the same time, Johnny was getting recognition for his songwriting

skills. Tammy Wynette's first hit, "Apartment #9," was written by Johnny, as was Ray Price's "Touch My Heart."

In 1965, with the release of "A-11," his solo career took flight. A string of Top 10 hits followed, including "11 Months and 29 Days," "Song & Dance Man," "Someone to Give My Love To," "Don't Take Her, She's All I've Got" (nominated for a Grammy in 1970), "Slide Off of Your Satin Sheets," and his own personal favorite, "Old Violin." For a period of eleven years, from 1970 to 1981, Johnny placed at least three singles on the country charts each year. But it was the rebellious anthem "Take This Job and Shove It," a worldwide crossover hit, that propelled Johnny to a level of superstardom achieved by only a few artists. The song not only sold millions of copies and made Johnny a household name, it also became the basis for a major motion picture.

With six gold albums and thirty-three hit singles, and one of the most distinctive voices in country music, Johnny PayCheck is a true living legend. He joined the cast of the Grand Ole Opry on November 8, 1997.

Johnny
Remembers . . .

A couple years ago around Christmastime I took my family down to New Orleans for a cruise in the Gulf of Mexico—just me and my wife and my son. We hadn't been on a cruise in a long, long time—probably about twenty-five years. My wife hadn't been feeling well, and my son was getting ready to leave school and take a job in Cincinnati, and I just felt like this was the right time to do something together as a family. After all the years of the hard living, and after leaving my wife home all the time to raise our son, this would be a great opportunity to show my appreciation for everything she'd done. I'd been through a lot in my life, and I'd put my family through a lot. Drugs . . . booze. Just about everything that a man could do, I'd done it. Financially, of course, I did take care of my family. But it wasn't easy for them. As for Christmas, well . . . we always had a nice tree and lots of presents and stuff. But I worked a lot, too. Sometimes I was gone on Christmas. Or I'd be gone all week and barely make it back in time. So I just felt a need to do something special.

Anyway, we got to New Orleans and boarded a ship. We sailed out into the Gulf of Mexico and cruised around for about a week. For me, it was a combination of work and relaxation. I did one show in the middle of the week, but mostly it was just a holiday vacation. We went through a couple storms, got a little seasick, but overall it was a real nice time. When we got back to New Orleans, the trip was supposed to end. But it didn't. Instead, I asked my wife if she'd like to go to Disney World. We'd gone there once before, about ten years earlier, and we'd had a great time. So, on the spur of the moment, I just said, "Let's take the money I just earned and head on down to Disney! Let's have a great week and just enjoy each other's company."

Johnny PayCheck

Unfortunately, I became ill when we got to Disney World. My health went downhill in a hurry. A week later I got out of bed for a New Year's Eve show in Nashville with Tim McGraw—against my doctor's wishes. Tim saw me in the dressing room that night and said, "John, you need to go home." But I wasn't about to leave. I did the show, and the crowd loved it. Afterward Tim gave me a big hug and I went home. A couple weeks later, while driving across the country for another show, I began having trouble breathing. Pretty soon I was in the hospital. In fact, I actually died on the table, but the doctors brought me back.

I've had some pretty bad health problems ever since, and I haven't worked as much as I'd like. But the thing that I remember the most about that whole period is the trip with my family. I'll never be able to repay them for everything they've done for me. But I'm glad I had the chance to take that Christmas vacation, because I might never get another chance.

The Grand Ole Opry Country Christmas Album

STU
Phillips

STU PHILLIPS WAS born in Montreal, a predominantly French-speaking city that's not exactly known for its love of country music. Stu, however, traveled west when he was still quite young and eventually took root in Calgary, Alberta. The atmosphere of the Canadian Rockies not only suited his personality but proved to be a wonderful muse as well. He began writing songs while in his teens and, whenever he could pull in the signal on his radio, listened to broadcasts from the Grand Ole Opry.

A true showman, Stu honed his craft through years of nonstop performing. Whether at a church or a club, or on one of his own radio or television programs, Stu could always be counted on to provide a thoroughly entertaining and polished show. An engaging man with a soulful voice and a warm personality, he was naturally suited to the intimacy of the small screen. Over the years Stu has appeared with a variety of stars, including Johnny Cash, Tennessee Ernie Ford and Danny Thomas. His long list of hit records includes "The Great El Tigre," "Juanita Jones," "Note in Box #9" and "Bracero." A compilation CD of his early songs was released in 1993 by Bear Family Records. An adventurous sort, Stu has traveled and toured throughout the world. (Interestingly, he's had several gold records in Africa.) In his spare time he obtained a divinity degree from the University of the South in Sewanee, Tennessee, and is now an ordained minister in the Episcopal Church.

Stu has been a member of the Grand Ole Opry since June 1, 1967, and a United States citizen since July 1998.

Stu
Remembers . . .

I'm an artist, and I see Christmas in a sensitive way. Religious symbols, icons are very meaningful to me. The symbols on Christmas cards that conjure up so many fond memories of my childhood. Hearing the story of Jesus for the first time, learning and singing Christmas carols, participating in school plays, things like that. When I think of Christmas and the days prior to the holiday, I'm almost certain I can smell the turkey roasting in the oven. So the nostalgia of Christmas is very meaningful to me. I truly look forward to the many sounds and images of Christmas, the great songs you hear at Christmastime, the sounds of tire chains in fresh snow, even the silent sounds, the serenity of Christmas Eve and Christmas Day. Then there is the special sound of bells, which is very, very meaningful to me, above all. For me, the meaning of Christ is summed up in the familiar ring of the bells of the Salvation Army. And for a very special reason.

This vignette takes place in 1939, when I was six years old in Canada, in Montreal, and my family had been devastated by the Depression. And for Canadians, we went right into preparation for World War II. We were part of the British Commonwealth, and the war in Europe started just about that time. My father was heading off to war, which was his first steady work in years. He had been an architect in large buildings, worked for the railway, but of course there was no building going on. It was two days before Christmas, and I remember Mom telling Dad that we had little, if anything, for Christmas that year. She cried, and I remember telling her it was okay, we'd get along all right, everything would be fine. I hated to see Mom cry at any time. Mom and Dad had known much better times before the Depression. They were both from good and

Stu Phillips

honorable families. Mom actually was from a crested family, and she was a very proud lady. I felt so very sorry for her.

I worked odd jobs. I delivered ninety newspapers every morning and afternoon, the Montreal Gazette, even though I was only six years old. And I gave Mom all the money, which was customary in those days. I wasn't expecting much for Christmas, and it looked as though my expectations were going to come true on that particular day. Things were very quiet around the house, until approximately 7:30 in the evening, Christmas Eve. Suddenly the doorbell rang, and we heard the glorious sound of Christmas bells, and the singing of carols. Mom threw open the door as if she was really expecting something. She was. It was the Salvation Army with boxes and boxes of gifts, and food for the holidays, even a turkey that was big enough to feed us for the week. Gifts included toys and candy and cake, and gifts for Mom and Dad, too. I recall what a wonderful Christmas it was, the most wonderful Christmas of all.

Years later, even now, I reflect upon that Christmas, recalling how very difficult it must have been for Mom to contact the Salvation Army. She had never asked for charity in all her life. Love was the motivating factor, I'm sure: love for her family, which is a selfless love for others. That's what the holidays are all about: selfless love, charity, and peace and goodwill for all, represented by the birth of the Christ Child.

Stu's
Favorite Christmas Songs

I guess I'd have to say mine is "Silent Night." I just love it. It's ageless, and it puts me in the mood for Christmas. And in the pop field, I guess "I'll Be Home for Christmas." I've traveled the road so many times, for so long . . . that song has a special connotation for me.

CHARLEY
Pride

❦ ⚬ ❦

ONE OF ELEVEN children born to poor sharecroppers in Sledge, Mississippi, Charley Pride overcame his humble roots to become one of the top-selling recording artists in history. Charley's resume includes thirty-six No. 1 singles, thirty gold albums and four platinum albums. He's sold more than thirty million records worldwide.

Charley grew up in a family that cherished music. He began singing with his brothers and sisters when he was just five years old, and bought his first guitar from Sears Roebuck when he was fourteen. Some of his earliest memories involve sitting alongside his father, listening to broadcasts from the Grand Ole Opry on a portable radio.

Charley's musical career began, oddly enough, while he was pursuing an entirely different line of work: professional baseball. As a player for the Memphis Red Sox of the Negro American League, Charley liked to sing and play guitar while riding on the team bus. As the team traveled around the country, Charley would often jam with other bands. During a trip to Nashville, Charley met producer Jack Clement, who arranged a recording session for him. Charley completed the session with a two-song demo, which led to a recording contract with RCA. His first single, "The Snakes Crawl at Night," was released in 1966, and suddenly Charley was on his way.

The ascent to stardom wasn't easy, of course. As one of the first African-American country singers, he had to break down barriers and overcome stereotypes. Ultimately, though, Charley's talent and perseverance paid off. His rich baritone became one of the most recognizable and beloved sounds in all of country music. Between 1969, when "All I Have to Offer You Is Me" hit No. 1 on the singles charts, and 1984, when "Every Heart Should Have One" reached similar heights, Charley placed nearly three dozen records at the top of the singles charts. Among his biggest hits were "Is Anybody Going to San Antone?" "I'm So Afraid of Losing You Again," "Mountain of Love" and "Kiss an Angel Good Morning," which sold more than a million copies and became a huge crossover hit with pop audiences.

Charley has been named *Music City News* Male Vocalist of the Year five times, Country Music Association Male Vocalist of the Year twice and CMA Entertainer of the Year once. He's also won three Grammy Awards. Charley was inducted into the Grand Ole Opry on May 1, 1993, and the following year received the Academy of Country Music's Pioneer Award. In 2000, he was inducted into the Country Music Hall of Fame.

Charley

Remembers . . .

*S*ome of my most vivid Christmas memories make me laugh now, even though they actually seemed kind of scary at the time. Up until we were five, six, seven, maybe eight years old, I remember my mother used to tell us kids on Christmas Eve, "If you don't go to sleep . . . if Santa sees you peeking . . . he's gonna put ashes in your eyes!" Now, I'd never had anybody do that to me, and I'd never seen it done to anyone else, but man . . . I thought about how ashes look coming out of that hearth. You know, we used to heat our house with it, and we baked potatoes and all that. So the thought of Santa taking ashes from that hearth and rubbing them in our eyes . . . well, that wasn't too good. Of course, I was pretty sure she was just trying to scare us into sleeping. Still, when we'd go to bed, I'd squeeze my eyes real tight and hope I could fall asleep as quick as possible—because as everyone knows, the quicker you go to sleep, the quicker Santa will show up.

When we'd wake up in the morning, my bag would be under the tree. My parents put everything in paper bags with our names on them. So I ran to the bag with "Charley, Jr." on it and opened it up. Even now, whenever I eat an orange or an apple or a banana, that's still my Christmas. All these years later, it just takes me right back to when I was a kid, and Christmas morning. That's the taste that takes me to Christmas, because that's the only time we got fresh fruit like that in our family. We lived in the country and we were really poor. Back then you couldn't just run to the fridge and grab an orange or an apple. It didn't work that way. That was a luxury to us.

Sometimes there were other presents. We'd get Roman candles and firecrackers. That made us happy a lot. And one time my older brother and I got a couple cap pistols. But gifts like that were rare.

Charley Pride

 155

I remember something else that seemed funny when I grew up, but was disheartening when I first heard it, and that was finding out the truth about Santa Claus. My mother came to me one day and said, "Let me tell you, son, Daddy and me are really Santa Claus." I don't think I was more than six or seven years old. And I know now she was just trying to soften the blow, but it hurt, man. I was shocked. I said, "What are you talking about? Santa Claus comes down through the chimney!" The first time around she didn't elaborate very much, just sort of put it out there for me to chew on. And I said, "Uh-uh. Santa's real. I even saw where he ate off the cake we left out for him." That night, just like always, I waited on that old man with the big fat belly and the red cheeks. I waited for him to come down the chimney the way he always did. And I wasn't disappointed. But when I got a little older and it finally dawned on me that my mother was telling me the truth, that really hurt.

The best part about Christmas when I was an adult was the happiness I was able to give my kids. I could give them so much more than my parents were able to give me. That's what made me joyous and happy and gratified, when I could see their eyes light up on Christmas morning. When my wife and I were able to make them that happy, just by giving them . . . not too much—well, some people might say too much, but we felt it wasn't overdoing it. That made me feel real good. It still does, in fact. We get together as much as we can, even though my kids are grown now. Oh, and one other thing. As far as telling my kids the truth about Santa Claus? I never did. I think they were smart enough, of course, what with TV and all that. I'm sure they just figured it out for themselves. But they didn't hear it from me.

DEL
Reeves

ONE OF THE more energetic and popular performers in Nashville, Del Reeves taught himself how to be a musician when he was just a small boy. He was the youngest of eleven children, and when his guitar-playing older brothers joined the service during World War II, Del began experimenting with the instruments they left behind. By the age of twelve he was playing and singing with a local band and performing regularly on a Saturday morning radio show.

After attending Appalachia State College and serving in the U.S. Air Force, Del began his professional recording career by signing a contract with Capitol Records. Although Del was based in California, rather than Nashville, he developed a reputation as a world-class writer and performer of country music. In 1962, at the urging of his friend Hank Cochran, Del moved to Nashville, and his career soon took off. His first big hit was 1965's "Girl on the Billboard," which sold more than a million copies for the United Artists label and reached No. 1 on the country charts. "The Belles of Southern Bell" was a Top 5 hit later that year, and "Women Do Funny Things to Me" reached the Top 10 the following year.

Del was invited to join the cast of the Grand Ole Opry in October of 1966. With his parents in the audience, and Porter Wagoner providing a heartfelt introduction, Del was so overcome with emotion that he began crying and had to cut short his performance.

Over the years Del has released more than two dozen hit singles, including "Looking at the World Through a Windshield," "Be Glad," "There Wouldn't Be a Lonely Heart in Town," "A Dime at a Time," "Philadelphia Fillies" and "Swinging Doors." He has also appeared in several motion pictures, including the 1969 release *Sam Whiskey*, starring Angie Dickinson and Burt Reynolds. Del also has hosted his own television show, *Del Reeves Country Carnival*.

$\mathcal{D}el$
Remembers . . .

One Christmas I remember well was when I was about six or seven years old. Of course, we didn't get a lot back then, when we were young, except maybe an orange and a tangerine. That was about our Christmas. We had 11 kids in our family, and I was the youngest one of all of them. Money was spread pretty thin, so we got very little. But when I was seven years old, I got a one-shot air rifle. You had to carry the BBs in your mouth, spit into the gun and then cock the gun, and it sucked the BBs down into the barrel. Boy, I'll tell you, I thought I was king of the mountain when I saw that gift. I had asked for it a long time ago, but hadn't got it, and wasn't expecting to get it. We were used to using slingshots, and of course, they weren't very accurate. Maybe one out of thirty times you shot at a can, you'd hit it.

Anyway, I took my new air rifle and went out a little while later, hunting for little birds or anything else I could find. I was out with my first cousin, and I saw this little yellow bird. "Try and shoot him!" my cousin yelled. It was just a little bitty thing. But I said, "Okay!" And I shot that rifle, and that little bird fell off a limb. I was all excited at first, but when I went to pick him up . . . my Lord! Something inside me just said, "This is wrong!" And I took that little bird and I left my cousin and went running back to the house.

I ran inside and yelled, "Mama, look what I done!" I started crying and everything. She said, "Don't cry, don't cry. We'll give it a good burial." So she put it in a shoe box and we buried that little bird. From that day on, I never shot another little bird. I was absolutely tore up. I talked to everybody about it; I was trying to get everybody to tell me it was all right, which they did. But I felt I'd done something unspeakable.

Del Reeves

To be honest, I never was a big hunter. As a matter of fact, after we made it in the business and moved to the country, my wife bought me a 30-30 rifle for Christmas. That morning, when I opened it up, all my little girls were there.

"Oh, boy," I said. "Now I can go deer hunting!"

And they said, "Oh, Daddy, you're not gonna shoot Bambi?!"

Needless to say, I've never fired that rifle. It's still in the rack.

Another Christmas I remember was when I was older and made the Grand Ole Opry. One of the first things I wanted to do was take care of my mama. She never had a washing machine or a refrigerator or a deep freeze or a stove.

Didn't have a TV, either. So I just furnished the whole house. I bought everything in November so that it would arrive by Christmas. I couldn't wait to do that, as soon as I had enough money. We surprised her, and she was so happy. She couldn't believe it. She said, "Why did you spend your money like that?" You see, back up in the hills of North Carolina, it was unimaginable that anyone could make $250 a day. That was unheard of. Only the bank made that much money. But I said, "Mama, I wanted to do it." It made me feel great to see her smile like that.

Del and Brad Paisley

The Grand Ole Opry Country Christmas Album

Del's
Favorite Christmas Song

My favorite Christmas song is one off an album I did in 1968. It's called "Santa Got Lost Somewhere." One of the things that makes it so special is that my wife wrote it.

Riders In The Sky

Ranger Doug
Woody Paul
Too Slim

THE POPULAR TRIO Riders In The Sky was formed in 1977 as a cheerful homage to traditional cowboy music and humor. In the spirit of such cowboy legends as Riders of the Purple Sage and Sons of the Pioneers, Riders In The Sky embrace smooth harmonies and expert musicianship. But their performances also are punctuated by rope tricks, slapstick comedy, droll punch lines and tongue-in-cheek frontier wisdom. ("Always drink upstream from the herd"; "Never squat with your spurs on.")

The trio consists of lead singer, songwriter and rhythm guitarist Ranger Doug; upright bass player Too Slim, who also writes the scripts for many of the trio's sketches; and

Woody Paul, the "King of the Cowboy Fiddlers," who sings lead and tenor. Interestingly, each member of the troupe thought long and hard about doing something else with his life. In fact, Riders In The Sky must be the most highly educated band in country music, if not all of popular music. Ranger Doug holds a master's degree in literature, Too Slim has a graduate degree in wildlife management, and Woody Paul has a Ph.D. in plasma physics from the Massachusetts Institute of Technology. But a passion for music and performing brought them together and keeps them on the stage.

Riders In The Sky released their first album, *Three on the Trail*, in 1980. Two years later they were invited to join the cast of the Grand Ole Opry on June 19. Since then they've released twenty-one albums, performed more than four thousand line shows and appeared on national television some two hundred times. With a repertoire that includes traditional cowboy favorites such as "Rawhide," "Cool Water" and "Tumbling Tumbleweeds," as well as an eclectic mix of original material (romantic ballads one minute, robust accordion music the next), the trio enjoys a spirited and devoted following that knows no age limits.

Since 1989 Riders In The Sky have hosted a weekly program, *Riders Radio Theater*, on National Public Radio. They've also starred in their own Saturday morning television series on CBS and hosted *Tumbleweed Theater* on The Nashville Network. Their music was also featured on the soundtrack of the hit 1999 film *Toy Story 2*.

Ranger Doug

Remembers . . .

There are a couple things I remember from my childhood at Christmastime. The first one involved the fact that I was apparently an active young fellow. And two years in a row I snuck down the stairs in the middle of the night and got so interested in the lights decorating the tree that I just couldn't resist . . . and so I ran over and grabbed the lights and pulled the tree over. Twice I did that.

The other thing happened when I was very young. I've been told this story many times, but the truth is I don't really remember it. But I'm sure it's true. I was a precocious little guy, and my parents were naturally very proud of the things I'd learned. Well, sometimes they trotted me out before the relatives to show them how much I had gathered about the meaning and spirit of Christmas. And one time they said, "All right, Douglas, tell everybody . . . who was born on Christmas Day?" And I stood there smartly and piped up, "Why, Little Douglas, of course!" Unfortunately, my real birthday is in March.

My other memories of Christmas revolve around being an adult, especially since I have five children. My kids were like most kids, I guess, always getting up early, way before the parents, sneaking downstairs and trying to scope out what was down there under the tree. You know, the gray dawn light streaming in, nudging each other in the side, giggling, saying, "Is that a bike? It is, isn't it?"

I'm the oldest of three kids, and we all make an effort to share Christmas. I'm fortunate because my brother lives here in Nashville, and we get together with our kids every year. We've made our own family connections and tradition even stronger than they were when we were growing up.

Ranger Doug's
Favorite Christmas Song

We just released a Christmas album, so I have a lot of favorites right now. The best tune on the album is an old one called "The Friendly Beast." It's based on the Christmas legend that animals speak once a year on Christmas Eve. Animals in the manger tell the story of how each of them took care of Baby Jesus. It's a beautiful old song; the Louvin Brothers did it beautifully, and we put three-part cowboy harmony to it, and I think it's the best thing on the record.

JEANNIE
Seely

WHEN SHE WAS a little girl growing up in Pennsylvania, Jeannie Seely dreamed of performing at the Grand Ole Opry. Her parents would often listen to the Opry radio broadcasts on Saturday nights while playing cards with friends. Jeannie would sit nearby, soaking it all in, imagining the day when people would come to see her perform.

For such a small girl in such a small town, Jeannie had grand ambitions. But she was much more than just a starry-eyed dreamer. Jeannie had talent and drive, and by the time she was eleven years old she was working toward achieving her goals. She started out by performing on a weekly radio show in Meadville, Pennsylvania, and later progressed to clubs and fairs and larger auditoriums. In 1965, at the urging of the Opry's Dottie West, Jeannie moved to Nashville and landed her first recording contract, with Monument Records. Jeannie's first hit record, "Don't Touch Me," not only broadened her audience, but also earned her a Grammy Award for Best Female Vocal Performance. She embarked on a worldwide tour, became a featured performer on the Ernest Tubb television show and in 1967 was invited to join the cast of the Grand Ole Opry on September 16.

Over the years Jeannie has had numerous country hits, including "Lucky Ladies," "Tell Me Again," "Little Things" and "I'll Love You More." She also paired with Jack Greene to form a hugely popular duet team whose hits included "Wish I Didn't Have to Miss You" and "You and Me Against the World." The pair received several Grammy nominations and even served as Music City's Goodwill Ambassadors to the annual United Nations banquet and concert in Washington, D.C. A gifted writer as well as a performer, Jeannie has penned songs for Dottie West, Willie Nelson and Ray Price, among others. More recently she has turned her attention to another lifelong ambition: acting. Jeannie's stage credits include roles in *The Best Little Whorehouse in Texas, Everybody Loves Opal* and *Always . . . Patsy Cline;* she also appeared in the film *Honeysuckle Rose.* But she remains, first and foremost, a singer. Jeannie still maintains a hectic touring schedule and can be seen regularly at the Grand Ole Opry.

Jeannie
Remembers . . .

It was either 1949 or '50, and I was either nine or ten years old. I wanted a Howdy Doody string marionette for Christmas. Now, at that time, that was a really expensive gift for our family. My dad worked in a steel mill in Pennsylvania. My mother never worked outside the home, but she worked very hard in the home—there were four children in the family. We never went hungry, we never went without clothes. It wasn't like I didn't have a coat or anything like that. I might have wished I had a newer one, but we were taken care of. My parents worked very hard and I know they both sacrificed a lot to make sure we had the things we needed.

Typically, for Christmas, we would get clothes, and usually my parents would strive to give us one other thing that we really wanted, if it was possible to get. And we'd get some smaller things, too . . . homemade things. I was taught to appreciate those kinds of gifts—I know a lot of people aren't. And I still appreciate them today, because I learned so many things from receiving them. In fact, that's a tradition I'm trying to carry on. We had a family reunion recently, and one of the things I did was take an old bookcase and paint it white. Then I added flowers and vines. My neighbor is an artist, and she taught me how to do it. So just for a fun family project we had that bookcase ready for painting, and we had everybody make their own little flower or vine or something on that bookcase. Well, my great-great-nieces are six and nine years old, and they just were so into it. It was wonderful to see their imagination. So I spent the summer shopping garage sales and yard sales looking for two small desks to give them for Christmas. I found them and painted them each white. And they'll get that for their rooms, along with a box to open. And in the box are paints and brushes and sponges.

Jeannie Seely

Now, it would have been a lot easier to go to Wal-Mart, but I prefer this because it's something for them. It's personal, and they can use their creativity on it.

Anyway, this brings me back to the marionette. I wanted this doll because The Howdy Doody Show *was popular then, and I was fascinated by the show business end of it. I said to my parents, "Don't get me anything else. I'll wear the same clothes, the same pajamas. If we can only afford one thing, I'd love to have a Howdy Doody puppet." And I got it. And I still have it. He is still in the original box he came in, along with the brochure of other marionettes you could order. The cost on one of them was $3.49. I don't know if that's what Howdy Doody cost, but I presume it was about the same. That was a lot of money then.*

But what really makes it interesting is what we did after I got the marionette. My girlfriends and I ended up making more puppets. We used balsa wood for the body, and we used papier-mâché for the head, and we just copied from this puppet. I remember making the faces. I remember dropping the strings through so the marionettes could move, just like Howdy Doody. I remember we made Dracula and Frankenstein, and a bunch of female puppets. Then we would make up stories about the characters, and we ended up performing them at school programs. We even got excused from classes to put on shows for the younger kids. It was wonderful! And it all grew out of this one gift.

Looking back, what made it so special was the creativity, and the fact that my life has always been show business. I can vividly remember my mother saying to friends, "I hope this kid can make a living with her imagination, because she's got more of that than anything else." And now that's pretty much how I make a living. So that's the one thing I remember more than anything else through all my childhood holidays, opening that box on Christmas Eve and seeing Howdy Doody. I was just thrilled.

Jeannie's
Favorite Christmas Song

My favorite Christmas song would have to be "I"ll Be Home for Christmas," because I do appreciate having a family. Through all the years when we were traveling so much, we often just barely made it home for Christmas. That's the hardest part of touring—being away from home during the holidays.

JEAN
Shepard

A S ANY YOUNG, aspiring artist would surely attest, there is nothing quite like having a set of understanding, supportive parents. Jean Shepard, who would go on to become a legitimate country music legend, was blessed that way. She was born in Pauls Valley, Oklahoma, and spent most of her childhood in Visalia, California. One of ten children in a family that appreciated and enjoyed music, she had little in the way of material possessions, but never lacked for love or kindness. When Jean was a preteen musician who wanted her own instrument, her parents pawned some of their furniture so that they could afford to buy her a stand-up bass.

Whether that was the gesture that launched Jean's career is debatable, but this much is clear: it was money well-spent.

As a high school sophomore Jean helped form an all-girl western swing band known as the Melody Ranch Girls. She sang and played bass for the group, which quickly attracted a local following through live performances and radio appearances. After watching the Melody Ranch Girls open for him one night, Hank Thompson was so impressed that he introduced Jean to record company executives. In 1952, at the age of nineteen, she signed a contract with Capitol Records. One year later she hit the top of the charts with "A Dear John Letter," which she recorded with Ferlin Husky. The duo also hit No. 1 with "Forgive Me, John." As a solo artist, Jean recorded more than twenty-five albums and had huge success with such songs as "Satisfied Mind," "Beautiful Lies," "Another Lonely Night," "Slippin' Away," and "Seven Lonely Days."

Jean was invited to join the cast of the Grand Ole Opry on her birthday, November 21, 1955. In 1963, her husband, Opry star Hawkshaw Hawkins, died in the plane crash that took the life of country superstar Patsy Cline. Jean was eight months pregnant with her second child at the time. When the boy was born, Jean named him after his father: Harold Franklin Hawkins II. Jean later married musician Benny Birchfield. The two still travel and tour extensively, backed by their band, the Second Fiddles.

Jean

Remembers . . .

I came from a family of sharecroppers in Oklahoma. I was one of ten children born to Hoyt and Allie Mae Shepard in 1933. Needless to say, we were very poor. I remember Christmas as a very special time of the year. We hardly ever got toys. Once in a while we might get something that Daddy had made for us, but never store-bought toys. Usually we would get an orange, an apple, a banana, nuts of some kind and several pieces of hard Christmas candy.

My mother was a wonderful cook, so we always had lots of kinfolk show up for Christmas dinner. My daddy's sister and her family came on this particular Christmas, and she had two daughters. For Christmas these girls had both gotten the most beautiful dolls we had ever seen. My aunt would not let them take the dolls out of the car. She was afraid that if we played with them, we would get them dirty. My sisters and I

Jean Shepard

wanted to hold those dolls so bad it hurt. I remember all of us standing and looking in the car windows at those beautiful dolls and wanting just to touch them, but not being allowed to. I thought at that time they were the luckiest kids in the world.

As I grew older, I realized that beautiful dolls and toys are not what Christmas is about. Christmas is a time for love and giving. A time for family and friends to express love and appreciation for one another and all the wonderful things God has given us. Most of all . . . His love. I also realize now that my aunt and her family did not share the love and closeness that my family did. As I look back, I think material things were more important to them, that "things" was what it was all about. I thank God every day for my wonderful family. I had the love of the greatest parents in the world. Now, when I look back on that Christmas, I can say with a heart full of love, "Thank you, Jesus, and happy birthday, Jesus. You are what it's all about."

Jean's
Favorite Christmas Song

My all-time favorite Christmas song is "Oh, Come All Ye Faithful." I just love the melody and I love what that song says.

DARYLE
Singletary

W HEN DARYLE SINGLETARY released his eponymous debut album in 1995, critics fairly gushed with praise. Lauded as "one of country's ever-dwindling number of arch-traditionalists" by *USA Today*, and a singer who "has a terrific presence and a knack for inhabiting a lyric" by *Entertainment Weekly*, Daryle seemed to have appeared out of nowhere as a fully developed performer and songwriter.

In truth, of course, he had spent years honing his craft. Daryle grew up in rural Georgia, where he sang gospel with family members and took voice lessons to improve his range. As a teen, he was a devout fan of country music, with Randy Travis, Keith

Whitley and George Jones among his favorite artists. Daryle worked for a while at a tractor dealership after graduating from high school, but moved to Nashville in 1990 in the hope of carving out a career for himself as a singer and songwriter. One night, while performing at the Broken Spoke, a club where he had a regular gig, Daryle was spotted by some members of Randy Travis's road crew. Impressed by his deep, rich vocals (which have drawn comparisons to Merle Haggard, Whitley and Lefty Frizzell) and his stage presence, they encouraged their boss to listen to one of Daryle's demo tapes. When Elizabeth Hatcher-Travis, Randy's wife and manager, heard the tapes, she wasted no time in offering the young singer a management contract.

Randy recorded one of Daryle's songs, "Old Pair of Shoes," and in 1995 Daryle signed with Giant Records. His first album was a critical and commercial smash, yielding the hit singles "I Let Her Lie" and "Too Much Fun," and leading *Country America* magazine to call him one of the Top Ten New Stars of 1996. His second album, *All Because of You*, was released in late 1996, and his third album, *Ain't It the Truth*, appeared in 1998. Both were warmly received by critics and consumers, a fact that makes Daryle proud. A neotraditionalist with a gravelly baritone, he is guided only by what he describes as an undying passion for country music.

"I've always said my music has to be simple, heartfelt," he says. "It's got to be close to the bone and related to gospel in that it's so sincere and honest. The country I grew up on is like that—it's true to real life. Three-chord kind of country, Jim Reeves–big kinda thing, swing country. To me, it's all country—and it's all pure. That's what it's supposed to be about."

Daryle
Remembers . . .

My favorite Christmas was when I was about twelve or thirteen years old. I grew up in Georgia, in a very conservative family. We were low- to middle-class, and growing up we didn't get really big presents. I wouldn't say we didn't get a lot of presents, but we didn't get big presents. Now, I had always ridden horses, ever since I was a little kid. But I'd never really had a horse that I could say, "This is mine. You gotta get off my horse now." We lived on a farm, and we always had at least one horse to ride, but I'd never had one that really belonged to me.

This particular year, we had borrowed a horse from a man down the road, a man my dad worked for. And I'd been riding this horse for a while, really getting along with him great, so I figured maybe Daddy would get this horse for me. Unfortunately, a couple days before Christmas we had to take the horse back, so here I am, twelve or thirteen years old, and I'm thinking, Man, here we go again. I'm not gonna get this horse for Christmas, just like every other Christmas. So we took the horse back, and I remember it was an unusual December, because it was cold and it was snowing. In south Georgia, even in December, you very seldom see snow, and it's usually not so cold that it freezes. But this was one of those unusual Christmases, and we had to leave the faucet running in the horse pen for the horse that we did have, so that she could have water. So I woke up on Christmas morning, and I opened my presents, and I was very thankful for what I did get. But still, in the back of my mind, I was thinking, Man, I wish I'd gotten that horse.

We always had breakfast at my grandmother's house on Christmas morning. It was a Christmas tradition. And so after we went through breakfast, we were all sitting around, and my daddy said, "Oh, my goodness! I forgot to turn the water off down in the horse pen, Daryle. Why don't you run down there and turn it off." Now, you have to understand that in the South it ain't nothing to see a ten-year-old or a twelve-year-old kid driving around in a pickup because there's nobody around to run over. So I jumped into the pickup and drove down there—the barn was probably about a mile from my grandmother's house—and as I pulled up, I saw the horse that we had taken back two days earlier. I was beside myself, just couldn't believe it. I ditched the truck, ran down there, saddled the horse up and rode her back to my grandmother's house. Just left the truck behind. I gave big hugs to everybody when I got back, because it was one of the most exciting days of my life. Finally, I had my own horse to ride. She was beautiful, a sorrel horse, a mare, and I named her Speckles because she had a few little white specks on her. And she was my first. Later, when I got a little older and started making some money on my own, I got another horse. When I moved to Nashville, unfortunately, I had to sell both of them, and I kind of lost track of them. But Speckles wasn't very old when I got her, so she's probably around somewhere.

Daryle's
Favorite Christmas Song

My favorite Christmas song is "Oh, Holy Night." I just love that song. I love the melody and I love everything it talks about. I think it explains the reason for the season better than any other song. I've always liked dynamic songs, and that's about as dynamic as you can get. It's absolutely a favorite of mine.

RALPH

Stanley

THE NEWEST MEMBER of the Grand Ole Opry, and the first to be inducted in the twenty-first century, is anything but a neophyte. In fact, with a career that stretches over a span of 50 years, and with more than 150 albums to his credit, Ralph Stanley is among the most prolific and respected artists in the annals of country music. Consider that no less a superstar than Bob Dylan once said "This is the highlight of my career" after performing alongside Ralph, and you get a pretty good idea of the man's stature within the music business.

Ralph was born in the Clinch Mountain region of Dickenson County, Virginia, and was taught the banjo by his mother. He and his brother, Carter Stanley, formed a band (appropriately named the Stanley Brothers, and backed by the Clinch Mountain Boys) that featured an eclectic mix of bluegrass, gospel and high-energy "square dance" licks. The Stanley Brothers started out at radio station WCYB in Bristol, Virginia. They built a large and loyal following through the 1950s and earned a reputation as one of the premier bluegrass bands. Sadly, in December of 1966, cancer took the life of Carter Stanley; he was just forty-one. Younger brother Ralph, grief-stricken and unsure that he wanted to perform without his partner and best friend, thought about retiring. Friends and fans, however, encouraged Ralph to carry on, and eventually that is what he did.

With his unmistakable high-lonesome vocals, and his exquisite work on the banjo, Ralph became not only one of the most respected and successful performers in country music, but an artist whose work was admired by that most demanding and difficult of audiences: other artists. Among the performers who have acknowledged Ralph's influence on their music are Dolly Parton, Dwight Yoakam, Bob Dylan and Emmylou Harris. He's also been a mentor to such gifted musicians as Ricky Skaggs, Larry Sparks, Keith Whitley and Charlie Sizemore, all of whom spent time in the Clinch Mountain Boys.

Ralph has received dozens of awards and honors. Among the most notable are: induction into the Bluegrass Music Association Hall of Honor (1992); a National Endowment for the Humanities Traditional American Music Award, presented by President Ronald Reagan in 1985; an honorary doctorate of music from Lincoln Memorial University; six Grammy Award nominations; and performances at the inaugurations of Presidents Jimmy Carter and Bill Clinton. An indication of Ralph's towering reputation within the country music world can be seen in his most recent project, *Clinch Mountain Country*, an album which features collaborations with an impressive list of thirty-four artists, including Alison Krauss, Hal Ketchum, Gillian Welch, Vince Gill, Bob Dylan, Ricky Skaggs and Joe Diffie. Ralph Stanley was inducted into the Grand Ole Opry on January 15, 2000.

Ralph
Remembers . . .

It was far from the best Christmas I ever had but it's the one I remember most. World War II had ended four months earlier, and I was arriving with the American occupation forces in Germany. I was an eighteen-year-old private in the U.S. Army, and this was the first holiday I had ever spent away from home. Actually, it was my first trip away from the mountains—period!

When I stepped off the ship at Bremerhaven, it was about five o'clock in the morning, and there was a big snow on the ground. I guess there were about a hundred other soldiers in my group, but I really didn't know any of them. I was really homesick. They had these big loudspeakers at the port, with music playing over them. The first thing I heard when I stepped off the ship was Roy Acuff singing "Not a Word from Home," a song written in 1942, not long after America entered the war. I cried when I heard it. The words seemed to be speaking directly to me.

After that I boarded one of these little "forty-by-eights," as they called them—a little boxcar train. All we had for heat was a big bucket with some coals in it. We rode about sixty miles and got off at this little town where we had Christmas dinner. We had turkey, I believe. But we didn't have a Christmas tree. The thing I remember best was getting a big Baby Ruth candy bar and a Pepsi-Cola. I really enjoyed that.

Ralph Stanley

TRAVIS
Tritt

IT'S NOT EASY to pin a label on Travis Tritt. The versatile entertainer from Georgia is one of the busiest stars in country music, seamlessly blending his interests in singing, songwriting, producing and acting to create a truly eclectic resume.

The son of James and Gwen Tritt was exposed to music at an early age, at first through his father's record collection (which featured the likes of Dolly Parton, George Jones and Buck Owens) and later through his participation in a church choir. He taught himself how to play the guitar at age eight, and by the time he was in his early teens, Travis knew he wanted to devote his life to music.

Like a lot of performers, of course, he endured some lean times. Travis spent nearly a decade on the honky-tonk circuit, writing songs and developing a distinctive sound (part country, part rock 'n' roll, part folk), before he landed his first record deal with Warner Brothers. When his debut album, *Country Club,* spawned a hit single of the same name in November of 1989, Travis was on his way. The album ultimately produced three No. 1 singles—"Help Me Hold On," "I'm Gonna Be Somebody" and "Drift Off to Dream." *Billboard* magazine named him Top New Male Artist in 1990.

Travis's second album, *It's All About to Change,* earned a pair of Grammy nominations in 1991. That same year he won the Country Music Association's Horizon Award and made his Grand Ole Opry debut. On February 29, 1992, he joined the Opry cast. In 1993 he won a Grammy for his collaboration with Marty Stuart and performed before a worldwide audience of a half-billion viewers during the Super Bowl.

With more than fifteen million albums sold, Travis is obviously a gifted and dynamic musician. But he's also an artist with a broad range of interests. In 1994 he published his autobiography, *Ten Feet Tall and Bulletproof,* and he's carved out a niche as a character actor in such films as *The Cowboy Way* and *Sgt. Bilko* and in the television shows *Touched by an Angel* and *Arli$$.*

Travis

Remembers . . .

When I was growing up, all of my Christmases were really wonderful. I have a younger sister, and our parents always went all out to make sure that we had a nice Christmas as kids. Looking back now, that makes me feel really fortunate, because I see so many people today who don't have that luxury.

We were lucky. My mother was a homemaker, and my father . . . well, we used to kid him. We'd say he was a jack-of-all-trades, and a master of none. He worked numerous jobs. He drove a potato chip truck for a while, he worked for the post office, he was the manager of a service station. He just worked like crazy, all the time.

We celebrated Christmas in our house I guess the way most families do. We looked forward to what Santa Claus was going to bring us. And we were never disappointed. But the one Christmas that stands out the most in my mind was when I turned fourteen years old. I was crazy about music by then. I'd been playing guitar since I was eight, and it was the most important thing in the world to me. I learned to play on a really crappy guitar. It was a very small guitar made by a discount company—not a name brand, not a Gibson or a Fender or anything like that. It was really a poor instrument. The strings were literally an inch and a half off the bridge, off the neck, and it was just so hard to play. So when I turned fourteen, and my dad asked me what I wanted for Christmas, I told him: "I want a twelve-string Epiphone guitar." And he said, "Son, you know, I'm not gonna get you anything that makes noise or that keeps you in your room. That's all you do now. You stay in your room all the time."

And he was right. I was completely enamored with learning new songs, learning more about guitars. I would sit in my room for hours with a little portable tape recorder,

trying to emulate some of the records I was listening to at the time: Red-Headed
Stranger, *by Willie Nelson,* An Evening With John Denver. *My tastes were all over
the place at the time, but I liked just about anything with a twelve-string guitar. I was
listening to Styx and James Taylor. I was listening to Boston—"More Than a Feeling"
started off with a twelve-string guitar. There was a lot of really cool stuff that used
twelve-string guitar.*

*My dad had grown up on country music, and he loved it. Nevertheless, being a musi-
cian was not what he had hoped that I would aspire to. He had hoped that I would be
one of those guys who would learn, as he had, to work on cars, to do things with your
hands to make a living. Something more practical. So the fact that I sang in church and
that I liked to play guitar and spend so much time with music really worried him. He
would say to me quite often, "I never met any musician in my life who ever amounted
to anything. Either they play music because they're too lazy to work or they're the kind
of people who end up drunk, with no money, doing drugs or whatever." Now, all the
musicians he had met were local-level musicians, but still . . . there was a lot of truth
to what he was saying. He knew how tough it was to break into the music business on
a professional level, and I think he wanted to protect me from the pain and disap-
pointment. That's why he didn't want to get anything that would encourage my interest in music. I knew he wanted me to learn how to hunt and go out and do all the things
that he loved to do as a kid, so eventually I said, "Okay, Dad, If I can't get a guitar,
how about a .22 rifle? Then we can go out and hunt rabbits together." And he agreed
to that.*

*Well, unbeknownst to me, about a week before Christmas, he and my mother were
sitting in the kitchen having coffee, and my dad said, "When we get done with breakfast, we need to go over to the music store."*

"Why?" my mother asked.

"Well, I've been thinking about it, and you know, Travis is not going to be happy with anything but that guitar. He's got his heart set on it."

That Christmas morning when I woke up, I completely expected there to be a .22 rifle under the tree, and I expected to go hunting later that day with my dad. You see, I had a bad habit at that time of sneaking around and looking for my presents. And I had found a box in the basement that contained a Winchester .22 rifle. So I assumed I had found my Christmas present. I knew it for a fact. What I didn't know was that my dad, who collected rifles, had bought that rifle for himself and tucked it away. So when I walked in and saw that guitar case under the tree on Christmas morning, I was completely, totally shocked. I couldn't believe it. Later that day I confessed to my dad that I had been snooping around and that I had seen the rifle box.

"That explains the look on your face," he said. I think he got a real kick out of seeing how surprised I was, and knowing that even though it was against his better judgment, he had gotten me exactly what I wanted. And it made my Christmas wonderful.

Travis Tritt

PORTER
Wagoner

Porter Wagoner, the flamboyant star of the Grand Ole Opry, is famous for his sartorial splendor. With his dazzling, sequined outfits, Wagoner is one of the original rhinestone cowboys, and even after more than a half century in show business, he still cuts a dashing figure onstage. In this case, though, clothes alone do not make the man. In fact, they don't even tell half the story.

The youngest of five children, Porter grew up during the Depression. He spent his early years on a farm in Howell County, Missouri, but later moved with his family to the town of West Plains. Porter began working to help support his family when he was only sixteen years old. One of his first jobs was as a grocery store clerk. When business was slow, Porter would play his guitar and sing just to pass the time. He was lucky to have a boss who not only enjoyed Porter's musicianship, but thought highly enough of it to sponsor a program on a local radio station that highlighted the boy's talent. In 1951 he jumped to a bigger station in Springfield, Missouri, and within just a few months he received an invitation to join Red Foley's *Ozark Jubilee*. He later became the featured singer on the nationally televised version of the show.

Porter first hit the charts as a songwriter, with "Trademark" (sung by Carl Smith) reaching No. 3 in 1953. He signed his first major recording contract two years later with RCA, and soon released his own No. 1 hit, "A Satisfied Mind," the first of nearly thirty singles he'd place in the *Billboard* Top 10. Among his hits were "Green, Green Grass of Home," "The Cold, Hard Facts of Life," "Misery Loves Company" and "The Carroll County Accident." Porter joined the cast of the Grand Ole Opry on February 23, 1957, and began hosting his long-running and immensely popular syndicated television series, *The Porter Wagoner Show*, in 1960. The show aired for twenty years and featured a number of talented musicians and comedians, the most famous of whom was a young singer named Dolly Parton. Parton became Porter's sidekick and singing partner in 1967. He not only helped launch her remarkable solo career, but also joined her on more than a dozen chart-topping duets, including the 1969 Grammy winner "Just Someone I Used to Know." The pair won the Country Music Association Vocal Group Duo of the Year awards in 1968, 1970 and 1971, and also earned three Academy of Country Music awards. Porter also won three Grammy Awards for his gospel collaborations with the Blackwood Brothers.

A multitalented artist and businessman with seemingly boundless energy, Porter has also been a successful record producer and publishing executive. His autobiography, *A Satisfied Mind: The Country Music Life of Porter Wagoner*, was released in 1992. In 1998 he was honored with the Living Legend Award at the TNN–*Music City News* Country Awards.

Porter
Remembers . . .

I remember Christmas when I was a little boy on a farm. My parents instilled in me that the meaning of Christmas was the birth of Jesus. We didn't have access to stores to shop for toys and so forth; however, my mom and dad would always decorate a tree that we cut down from off our farm.

Mama would sew popcorn and string it around the tree and tie ribbons on the tree. We'd always make fudge and Mom would have Dad pick up fruit from town. We'd usually get a new pair of shoes for winter every year. We would sing songs such as "Silent Night." Later in my life I wrote a song reminiscent of that time. The song was entitled "Happy Birthday, Jesus." I feel I was very fortunate to have a mother and dad who would instill in me and my brothers and sisters the true meaning of Christmas.

Porter Wagoner

201

CHARLIE
Walker

COUNTRY SWING IMPRESARIO Charlie Walker grew up on a cotton farm near Dallas. Thanks in large part to his father's interest in music, Charlie began honing his voice when he was just a teenager. Before he'd even graduated from high school, he was a regular performer at a Dallas club. Not long after that he signed on as a vocalist with the Cowboy Ramblers, a western swing band fronted by Bill Boyd. Only a year after joining the Ramblers, though, Charlie was summoned into military service. While stationed in Japan, he started working as a disc jockey with the Armed Forces Radio Network. It's safe to say that Charlie was chiefly responsible for introducing country music to a Japanese audience.

After his discharge, Charlie returned to the United States and settled in San Antonio, where he quickly built a reputation as one of the nation's most popular country music disc jockeys. He was inducted into the Federation of International Country Air Personalities Disc Jockey Hall of Fame in 1981.

While he was building a radio career, Charlie also found fame as a country singer. He's recorded more than thirty-five albums and placed nearly fifty songs on the national charts. Among his biggest hits were the million-seller "Pick Me Up on Your Way Down," "Tell Her Lies and Feed Her Candy," "Little Ole Wine Drinker Me," "Don't Squeeze My Sharmon" and "Truck Driving Man." Charlie was inducted into the Grand Ole Opry on August 17, 1967. In addition to his performances at the Opry, he appears frequently in Las Vegas and Reno. An accomplished golfer who still shoots in the seventies, Charlie participates in some of the biggest pro-celebrity tournaments in the country. He is also an ambassador to the Shriners Children's Hospitals.

Charlie

Remembers . . .

In 1995, the Scottish Rite Masons elected me to the Thirty-Third Degree of Scottish Rite Masonry, which is the highest degree you can get. I'm the fourth country music person to ever get it. The first was Gene Autry, the second was Roy Rogers, the third was Roy Acuff. And then me. It was quite an honor. I'd been active in it for many, many years, and it was very important to me. They were gonna have a coronation here in Nashville, around Christmastime, about a week before Christmas, and I thought this would be a good opportunity to get all my children together and let them share in it with me. I have ten children and they're scattered all over the country. But I just said, "I'll fly all you guys in here for this so you can go to the banquet with me the night I'm coronated."

Anyway, it was on a Saturday night, and knowing that they were all going to be here, I talked with the management of the Grand Ole Opry, and I said, "Since I'll be doing a late show that night, how about if I introduce all my children in the order in which they were born, and bring them out and let them sing 'White Christmas' with me, since it's just a week before Christmas." Why "White Christmas"? Well, it's one of my favorite Christmas songs. Of course I love all the old carols, but "White Christmas" . . . I had just gotten started in the music business in Dallas about the time that song became so big. And naturally I guess if you had to name a song, other than Christmas hymns like "Silent Night," I guess it would be the most popular Christmas carol of all time. That's why I chose it—that and the fact that it was something my kids all knew. That was important, of course, since they were going to be singing with no book. They all knew the song and they thought it was a great idea. They got a big kick out of the idea of coming out and being introduced. And the management said, "Boy, that'll be great." So that's

Charlie Walker

what we did. They flew in and went to the banquet and then out to the Opry House. I brought them out in the order in which they were born, from age forty-five down to sixteen, and the audience . . . well, ten children, that's almost unheard of these days. So the audience loved it, just went crazy. They thought it was just fantastic. And I got the names all right. I admit I have to think twice on my grandkids, but my kids . . . no problem there. I'm very fortunate. I have ten beautiful children. They weren't all by the same wife—in fact, they were by three different wives—but that's just the way it goes. The important thing is, they're all very healthy and successful, and they all love each other very much, which makes me very proud.

Christmas was always a big time of the year around our house. It was great. I look back on it now, even though they're grown, and I can remember so many things. The images kind of get blurred together, because it was such a big family, but I can remember this one getting his first bicycle, this one getting a sled, or whatever. So many smiles, so many great memories. See, I grew up in very hard times, during the Depression. We didn't get a whole lot. A package of firecrackers, maybe a cap pistol, a little fruit, stuff like that. It was hard times all over the country. So when I got to where I had some success, I tried to give my kids as good a Christmas as I possibly could. That was important to me. They've all had some great Christmases, and I still look forward to it. We're all spread out now, but we try to get as many of us together as possible every year.

STEVE
Wariner

WIDELY REGARDED AS one of the finest musicians, singer/songwriters/ producers in country music, Steve Wariner was born on Christmas Day, in Noblesville, Indiana. He began playing bass in his father's country band at the age of ten. While still in his teens, he caught the eye of Dottie West, who was so impressed that she invited Steve to play bass in her band. Through Dottie, Steve was introduced to the Grand Ole Opry, where he made his debut at the age of seventeen.

Steve refined his craft alongside not only Dottie West, but also Bob Luman and Chet Atkins, who signed him to a contract with RCA Records in 1977. Steve's solo career took flight with a remake of Luman's "Lonely Women Make Good Lovers," "Your Memory" and "By Now." He hit No. 1 in 1981 with "All Roads Lead to You." In 1985 Steve switched to MCA Records, where he put together a string of hits, including "Some Fools Never Learn," "You Can Dream on Me," "Where Did I Go Wrong," "Life's Highway" and "Small Town Girl."

Steve earned Grammy and Country Music Association Awards for "Restless," his 1991 collaboration with Mark O'Connor, Vince Gill and Ricky Skaggs, and he received wide critical acclaim for his self-produced album, *No More Mr. Nice Guy*, which showcased Steve's virtuosity on the guitar. He's had thirty Top 10 singles and more than a dozen No.1 singles. In 1998, his "Holes in the Floor of Heaven" took both Single and Song of the Year honors at the CMA's. But perhaps the highlight of his career came on May 11, 1996, when he joined the cast of the Grand Ole Opry, thus fulfilling a dream he had harbored since childhood.

A true Renaissance man, Steve is an accomplished painter as well as a singer, songwriter and producer. But he considers himself to be, first and foremost, a student of the six-string guitar.

Steve

Remembers . . .

I grew up at 892 South 8th Street, Noblesville, Indiana. Great memories from that address will never be forgotten. I remember the train came right down the middle of the street next to our house. And it snowed a lot every winter. I remember my mom bundled me up in so many layers of clothing I could barely breathe or move at all. I swear it seems like the winters back then were always colder and snowier. Aren't winters much milder these days, or is that just a distortion of a childhood memory?

I loved living that close to those railroad tracks. There's a stretch of 8th Street where it's not uncommon to look up and see that train coming right at you! It might have been only two or three miles per hour, but it could still be frightening. In the summertime, the caboose man would throw lollipops at all of us as we lined the sidewalks. Believe me, we knew what that whistle meant.

Every year, shortly after Thanksgiving, there was (and still is) a big Christmas parade. The most exciting part was always the arrival of Santa Claus. I remember seeing him riding up there on a bright, red, shiny fire truck. I would have bet my bicycle he was looking directly at me and waving. Santa would always be available to visit with all of the boys and girls in his little candy cane house on the square downtown, sitting there in the shadow of our beautiful old Victorian courthouse. Christmas carols could always be heard coming from the clock tower.

Not long ago my mother pulled an old G.I. Joe from her cedar chest and handed it to me with a smile. It was the sailor G.I. Joe I had received one Christmas Day in the mid-1960s—the very first year they were introduced. My mind immediately drifted back to that morning, running toward the tree, opening the box and seeing G.I. Joe with his sailor cap and duffel bag. As I was reminiscing, the years melted away. Suddenly, though, my mother snatched the doll from my hands and once again tucked it safely away in her cedar chest.

Oh, well . . .

It's always special going back home to Noblesville, particularly at Christmastime. I find myself keeping an ear out for those Christmas carols, and watching closely for that train!

CHELY
Wright

CHELY WRIGHT WAS three years old when she first declared her career aspirations at a holiday gathering of friends and family. A relative who was taping the event put a microphone in front of Chely and asked the little girl what she wanted to be when she grew up. The children around her had provided the standard answers: fireman, doctor, nurse. But Chely had stardom on her mind already. She yanked the microphone out of her interviewer's hand and proclaimed, loudly and enthusiastically, "I'm gonna be a country star!" She then proceeded to belt out the lyrics to "Hey, Loretta."

It would take some time and more than a little hard work, but eventually Chely Wright would make good on that promise. Raised in a family of musicians, Chely was singing professionally by the time she was eleven, and in her early teens fronted a band called Country Line. As a high school junior she was even offered a chance to sing on Missouri's *Ozark Mountain Jubilee*.

Chely's first big break came at age eighteen, when she became a cast member of the *Country Music USA* show at the Opryland theme park in Nashville. While there, Chely refined her singing and stage presence by taking on the personas of such country luminaries as Loretta Lynn, Jean Shepard and Minnie Pearl. Through her work at Opryland, Chely made contacts with producers Harold Shedd and Barry Beckett, who backed her debut album, the honky-tonk-flavored *Woman in the Moon*. That album yielded a popular single, "He's a Good Ol' Boy," and led to Chely's being named Best New Female Vocalist by the Academy of Country Music in 1994. Sales of the album, however, were unimpressive, and Chely spent the better part of the next eighteen months on the road, refining her performing skills while touring with the likes of Alabama, Tim McGraw and Alan Jackson. She resurrected her recording career in 1996 with the release of *Right in the Middle of It*, an emotional album that highlighted Chely's powerful singing voice. That led to a contract with MCA Nashville and the release of the 1997 album *Let Me In*, which featured the hit single "Shut Up and Drive."

In 1999 Chely delivered *Single White Female*, an intensely personal album that boasted performances by some of Nashville's most respected artists, including Alison Krauss, Vince Gill, Patty Loveless and Trisha Yearwood. The album's title track gave Chely her first No. 1 hit and became her first gold-selling album.

Chely
Remembers . . .

*A*s I get older, I realize more and more how precious one certain Christmas was. I think I realized it a little bit when I was a kid, but now that I've grown up, I really appreciate my eighth Christmas. Kids, of course, want presents for Christmas. Well, this particular year, my parents told us, I guess in early December, "Hey, it's slim pickings and we're not going to be able to get you any presents this year." And, of course, us kids thought, Yeah, right. But we had no money at the time. My dad was a union construction worker, and he was low man on the seniority pole, and there was bad weather, and he was the last man to get called for work. It was just a very lean year. I grew up in a rural community where nobody had any money to speak of anyway, but when my parents broke this news to us, we really didn't believe it. My brother and sister and I—we're all one year apart in age—we just said, "Aw, they're trickin' us. It's gonna be a good Christmas."

As it turned out, on Christmas morning, there were a few presents under the tree, and when we opened them up, we discovered they were all homemade presents. Mom had sewn us each a pair of pajamas, and they had made a couple of little dolls. And they made each of us a puppet. It had sticks on top, and long yarn legs, and big Styrofoam hooves. I think they were supposed to be reindeer, but I'm not sure. They were big, though. About four feet tall. And beautiful. We would stand off the back of the stairs and do puppet shows with them. I kept mine for a long time, well into my teenage years. I would look at it, and the older I got, the more I would appreciate the time and effort and love and thought that went into making that gift.

It was probably one of the more special and memorable Christmases we had. At first,

Chely Wright

when I opened the box, I didn't know it was a homemade gift. I was confused. And then I was excited, because it was such a big, beautiful puppet. But the minute I found out it was a homemade gift, just being a dumb little kid, I got sad. I wasn't disappointed, just worried. It upset me to know that we didn't have any money. I was worried about whether we'd have enough to eat. Of course, it never got that bad, but the realization that money doesn't grow on trees, to an eight-year-old kid, can be kind of disturbing.

As I grew up, though, I learned the value of a dollar. And these days, as I look around, I don't know anyone personally who can't afford to get their kid a gift. I really don't. I know people who are pretty strapped, and there have been times in my life when I wasn't sure how I was going to pay for the groceries, but I don't know anyone who is in the situation I was in that one Christmas. But I know they're out there. And the memory of that Christmas always inspires me to go pick an angel off the angel tree and buy a present and leave it. I mean, I know what Christmas is about—the birth of Jesus Christ. But Christmas was such a magical time for me as a child, and it makes me want to shower every kid I know with presents and candy and attention and Santa Claus Is Coming to Town movies, and all that stuff. That's important to kids. So it will always mean a lot to me that my parents sat down and said, "Hey, what can we do to keep this special? How can we make it magical for the kids, even though we don't have any money?"

Chely's
Favorite Christmas Song

I love "Silent Night." I think it's a timeless melody. I've heard so many arrangements of it. It can be done jazz and rock 'n' roll and country. It doesn't matter—it's always a beautiful song. When you put all the kids in bed and sit at your tree on Christmas Eve, waiting on Santa Claus . . . that silence is really beautiful.

TRISHA
Yearwood

ONE OF THE Grand Ole Opry's newest members (she was inducted on March 13, 1999) is also one of its hottest. With her exquisite voice and seemingly flawless taste in material, Trisha Yearwood has in recent years enjoyed the type of crossover success few artists ever achieve. Her greatest-hits album, *Songbook*, debuted at No. 1 in 1997 and produced three consecutive No. 1 singles: "How Do I Live," "In Another's Eyes," and "Perfect I Love." It was "How Do I Live," in particular, that launched Trisha into the stratosphere. The song was featured on the soundtrack of the movie *Con Air*, and while the film was not exactly revered by critics, Trisha's vocal work was. She performed the song at the Country Music Association show and picked up the

Female Vocalist of the Year award. The song also was nominated for an Academy Award, and Trisha's performance was one of the highlights of the Oscar telecast. Still riding a wave of popularity for *Songbook*, Trisha won another CMA award in 1998, as well as the Academy of Country Music's Top Female Vocalist award. She also took home a pair of awards at the Grammys.

After working as a receptionist at MTM Records, Trisha became one of the most sought-after demo singers in Nashville. While working on her record deal with MCA Records, Trisha sang background vocals on Garth Brooks's second album, *No Fences*. This led to her becoming his opening act on his 1991 tour, which put her in front of his massive crowds simultaneously with the release of her first album, *Trisha Yearwood*. Her first single, "She's in Love with the Boy," went to No. 1, and the album became the first debut album from a female country artist to sell more than one million copies. A string of hits followed, and by the mid-1990s Trisha was among the most popular artists in country music. Her astonishing rise to prominence was chronicled in the 1994 book *Get Hot or Go Home: Trisha Yearwood and the Making of a Nashville Star*. In both 1997 and 1998, she was named Female Vocalist of the Year by the Country Music Association.

Trisha
Remembers . . .

First of all, Christmas, for me, is definitely all about family. I'm real close to my mom and dad, and my sister. So Christmas to me is mainly about being together with them, being wherever they are, regardless of where it may be. It doesn't always have to be at my parents' house in Georgia. There have been times when I've gone there, and other times everyone has come to my place or my sister's. It really doesn't matter, as long as we're together.

As for my favorite Christmas memory, well . . . ever since I was little and knew that I wanted to be a country music singer, I had this dream, like everybody else does, I guess. You know, the fantasy is that you hit it big and after you release your first single you're rich. And of course we all know now that's not quite the way it works. But anyway, the fantasy is . . . What's the first thing I'm going to spend my money on? For me, the dream was to drive up in my parents' driveway in a brand-new Chevy truck for my dad. I'd have my album in the CD player and all that, and then I'd get out of the car and hand him the keys. That was the plan. That was the dream. Reality was something else, of course. The first single came out and I was still broke, so I couldn't exactly afford a new truck. But I did do it eventually. It was about a year or two after I got my record deal and my career was really starting to pick up. So I decided to buy my father something he'd remember. He'd been a Chevy guy for twenty-something years, and he had an old Chevy truck that he refused to trade in, even though it was rusting out and everything. He just wouldn't buy himself a new truck. So right before Christmas I went out and bought it for him. That was the first time in my life I ever did anything like that—you know, just wrote a check for something expensive. I walked into the showroom, told the salesperson what I wanted, and walked out with a beautiful, brand-new, black Chevy four-by-four truck for my dad.

My sister and her daughter came along with me on the ride to my parents' house. We drove down on Christmas Eve, and the really cool thing—in fact, it doesn't even sound like it could be real—is that it actually started to snow in Georgia. My mom and dad live in Monticello, a little town about an hour south of Atlanta, and the snow was getting heavier as we got closer. Anyway, we drove on, me behind the wheel, my sister and her little girl in the back. When my parents saw the headlights coming down the road, they stepped out into the driveway to meet us. I pulled up into the carport, got out of the truck, and handed my dad the keys. He had this surprised look, like he didn't know what to think. I'm sure when he first saw us coming he figured that I had bought myself a truck. But when I gave him the keys, he didn't say anything. He just shook his head. Then he smiled, and I could see he had a tear in his eye.

"It's for you, Dad," I said. And he gave me a big hug.

That was the best feeling in the world, making him happy. His daughters were home for Christmas, which was what he wanted most, of course. But to be able to give him that present on top of it . . . My dad is a retired banker, and he's one of those people who has always provided for his children. He's been a great provider. He's always taken care of us. So it's always been hard for him to accept gifts. But this time he couldn't say no. He had to accept it. It was a wonderful moment. That was about seven years ago, and he's still driving that truck.

Trisha's
Favorite Christmas Music

I love Christmas and I have, like, thirty Christmas CDs. The day after Thanksgiving I pop the Christmas CDs into the player and let 'em run. I love the spirit of the season. But I don't really have a favorite. I like all the traditional songs and when I made my own Christmas album, I did a mix of traditional songs and less-known stuff. One of my favorites is "The Christmas Song." You know, "Chestnuts roasting on an open fire . . ." Because it's simple and expresses that sentiment about what Christmas is like. The smells in the air . . . the way it feels.

Create a new family holiday tradition
at the Grand Ole Opry.®

This holiday season visit the cornerstone of country music and you'll find the spirit of the season. Nashville celebrates with magical holiday productions, and the world-famous Grand Ole Opry celebrates with country, bluegrass, comedy and more! At Opryland, experience a performance at the BellSouth Theatre or aboard the *General Jackson*. Enjoy a stay at the Opryland Hotel where more than two million lights are aglow every night. Finish your shopping with a trip through Opry Mills. Downtown, don't miss *A Musical Christmas Carol* at the historic Ryman Auditorium and a special holiday meal at the world-famous Wildhorse Saloon.

GRAND OLE OPRY

FOR TICKETS AND INFORMATION, CALL (615) 889-3060 OR LOG ON TO WWW.OPRY.COM

A GAYLORD ENTERTAINMENT COMPANY